T0377529

ADVENTURES IN BACKYARD GARDENING

Copyright © 2025 by Ron Smith

Library of Congress Control Number: 2024942486

All rights reserved. No part of this work may be reproduced or used in any form or by any means—graphic, electronic, or mechanical, including photocopying or information storage and retrieval systems—without written permission from the publisher.

The scanning, uploading, and distribution of this book or any part thereof via the Internet or any other means without the permission of the publisher is illegal and punishable by law. Please purchase only authorized editions and do not participate in or encourage the electronic piracy of copyrighted materials.

"Schiffer Kids" and the Schiffer Kids logo are registered trademarks of Schiffer Publishing, Ltd. Amelia logo is a trademark of Schiffer Publishing, Ltd.

Designed by Jack Chappell
Cover design by Lisa Smith
Illustrations by Lily Smith
All photos by the author unless otherwise noted
Retro white paper index card isolated on white with copy space for your message (page 77, bottom): © by Karen Roach, courtesy of www.shutterstock.com
The soil is white fungus. Abstract background (page 89, top): © wararara, courtesy of www.shutterstock.com

Type set in Frutiger/Yonder/True North

ISBN: 978-0-7643-6883-7
ePub: 978-1-5073-0521-8
Printed in China

Published by Schiffer Kids
An imprint of Schiffer Publishing, Ltd.
4880 Lower Valley Road
Atglen, PA 19310
Phone: (610) 593-1777; Fax: (610) 593-2002
Email: info@schifferbooks.com
Web: www.schifferkids.com

For our complete selection of fine books on this and related subjects, please visit our website at www.schifferbooks.com. You may also write for a free catalog.

Schiffer Publishing's titles are available at special discounts for bulk purchases for sales promotions or premiums. Special editions, including personalized covers, corporate imprints, and excerpts, can be created in large quantities for special needs. For more information, contact the publisher.

ADVENTURES IN
BACKYARD
GARDENING

— RON SMITH —

ILLUSTRATIONS BY LILY SMITH

**INSPRIRING YOUNG GARDENERS
TO GROW THEIR OWN FOOD**

Schiffer **Kids**®

4880 Lower Valley Road, Atglen, PA 19310

DEDICATION/ACKNOWLEDGMENTS

This book is dedicated to my family and friends who have shaped and shared my garden adventures.

To my grandfather: thank you for my first lessons in gardening. I will always cherish the memories of the salt air, the moist soil, and harvests shared with you and Grandmom.

To my great friend Dr. Ryan Rebozo, who has balanced his passion and study of nature and gardens better than anyone I know: I look forward to our next adventure together.

To Dr. Dave Goulson: thank you for reading my manuscript and providing your inspiring foreword and for your tireless work connecting gardens, nature, biodiversity, and people.

To Russell and Linda: your friendship, like your gardens, inspires me to plant the next season.

To Ann Charles, my editor, and my friends at Schiffer Publishing: thanks for your patience, guidance, talents, and confidence in the *Adventures*.

To my family: our shared gardens represent our life together—always exciting, practiced with love and respect, and full of surprises. I love you, Lisa, Lily, and Gabriel.

CONTENTS

No matter how many times I walk or work the same land, there is always something new to discover . . . that is my reward.

–GENE LOGSDON, AUTHOR OF *LETTER TO A YOUNG FARMER*

FOREWORD

DAVE GOULSON

SCIENTIST, CONSERVATION BIOLOGIST, GARDEN ENTHUSIAST, AND AUTHOR OF *THE GARDEN JUNGLE, A BUZZ IN THE MEADOW,* AND *GARDENING FOR BUMBLEBEES*

For a hundred years or more, we have grown steadily more detached from nature, forgetting that we are just one of millions of species on our planet, and that our survival depends on maintaining the health of our world's ecosystems. We have cleared pristine forests that once brimmed with life, damaged and eroded soils by plowing, and sprayed toxic pesticides that poisoned our soils and rivers. Many of us moved to live in cities and came to think that food appeared miraculously, shrink-wrapped in plastic, on supermarket shelves. As Rachel Carson wrote in *Silent Spring*, "[Humankind's] war against nature is inevitably a war against himself."

At long last, I think the tide is turning. There is a growing recognition that we need to learn to cherish our planet—it is the only one we have. Some farmers are exploring ways to manage without pesticides by encouraging natural enemies of crop pests, and finding ways to farm without regular plowing. These new regenerative farming systems are trying to work with nature, rather than fighting against it. In our towns and cities, a growing number of us have come to see our gardens as places where we can reconnect with nature, experience the joy of growing flowers and food, watch bumblebees and ladybugs, and listen to birdsong. By taking some simple steps to make our gardens nature-friendly, we can support literally thousands of wild species and ensure that our children grow up familiar with the sights and sound of buzzing bees and the flashing colors of butterflies' wings. Gardens are also a place where our children can learn about where real food comes from, experience the magic of germinating seeds, watch bees pollinate, and discover the simple joys of digging up potatoes and eating fruit straight from the tree.

Ron Smith and I share a crazy dream. Imagine that every garden, city park, urban green space, and road verge was managed to encourage wildlife. We could invite nature in to live in our cities, towns, and villages, turning them into verdant green oases of life. Crazy it may be, but slowly, garden by garden, it is happening . . .

INTRODUCTION

Some of the most important discoveries in the natural sciences occurred in gardens. In the 1800s, Gregor Mendel, an Austrian monk, planted peas in the abbey garden and ultimately established the basic foundation of inheritance: how information is passed on from one generation to the next. Around the same time, Charles Darwin, best known for his book *On the Origin of Species*, spent many years exploring, observing, and experimenting in his family's garden, developing ideas about how species are connected to their environment. In fact, Darwin spent many more years investigating his garden than the far-off places he visited on his famous expedition on the HMS *Beagle*! Studying earthworms, weeds, soil, and bees, Darwin made observations in his garden that contributed immensely to his own understanding of natural selection and to our modern knowledge of a variety of garden topics.

Many famous writers have been inspired by their gardens as well. Beatrix Potter, the author who brought the world *The Tale of Peter Rabbit*, was a lifelong gardener and developed so many of her characters and stories based on garden themes. Her life outdoors and details of her garden can be explored in *Beatrix Potter's Gardening Life* by Marta McDowell. Emily Dickinson, a famed American poet, wrote extensively about gardens and nature. From insects to plants to birds, her poetic creations reveal a connection to the natural world born out of simple observations and time spent in her home garden.

A backyard garden

Discoveries are still being made in gardens, and many of our modern conservation themes, from protecting biodiversity to addressing climate change, bring gardens into focus. Scientist and writer Dave Goulson establishes that the planet can actually be saved through study and practice in our gardens in his book *The Garden Jungle or Gardening to Save the Planet.*

Explorations, discoveries, and surprises await you in your garden. Investigating seed and seedling growth, composting, water conservation strategies, enhancing and protecting backyard biodiversity, and supplying nutritious additions to your dining experiences are all in store. In addition, gardens build community, connecting us with nature, our family, and our friends. We can embrace the form and function of every element of our flower beds and vegetable plots, all while being inspired to document, write, and wonder. Is there a better way to teach our children about the magic of nature and the need for sustainability than to be in the garden?

Whether you choose to tend a few pots of herbs from the windowsill of your kitchen or you endeavor to grow a season's worth of food for your family on a half-acre plot, you will have made the choice to join the garden adventure!

Chickens can be a great addition to a backyard garden.

PART ONE

GARDENING FOR PEOPLE
AND THE PLANET

— CHAPTER 1 —

EARLY DAYS OF A YOUNG GARDENER

Warm, salty air blew in from the bay through the open window in the kitchen. I placed my glass on my napkin to keep it from fluttering to the floor. The table was crowded with bowls and serving trays—a typical meal at my grandparents' house. They had prepared a meal for twice the number of people who would be dining. My brother and I were visiting Long Beach Island for a few days as we did several times each summer. Though we loved going to the beach and visiting the 5 and 10, we most celebrated spending time with our Gram and Pop.

I pose with my grandfather in the garden.

We thoroughly enjoyed the stories my grandfather would tell, and they did not need to be embellished to keep our attention. The events of his life and his time spent as a young person amazed us. Born in 1910, he was one of four children, all of whom had to help make ends meet in their home. He tended chickens, grew crops of many types, bartered with the neighbors for other food items such as milk and meat, and made many of his own tools—all around the age of fourteen! The most impressive feat, which amazes me to this day, was that he built his family's first refrigerator. Digging a deep well in the back garden, he lined it with stones and then built a pulley system used to lower and raise a sturdy wooden box that would keep dairy and meats cool enough to last a few days. To my brother and me, he could do anything!

The pasta dinner that he and my grandmother prepared was the standard first meal we would all share when my brother and I arrived, and it always included a gigantic salad served in a large wooden bowl. Every food item in that bowl came from my grandfather's garden. Despite the fact that there was enough to feed our extended family, nothing went to waste. When we ate with my grandparents we never hurried, but once we finished, my brother and I took on our post-meal jobs with enthusiasm. We were in charge of clearing the table and securing the leftovers (to be eaten tomorrow for lunch), and we were careful to put every scrap of bread or vegetable item that would not be saved into the compost bucket, always occupying the right side of the sink basin. Carrot peelings, fibrous broccoli stalks, and spinach roots from the pre-meal preparation were added to the day's coffee grinds and eggshells. The compost bucket nearly full, I grabbed the handle and, with a well-practiced swing, brought the bucket to my side and walked to the back porch.

My grandparents' victory garden

Pop's garden hat

Opening the screen door, I entered the garden. On the edge of the brick patio that had many raised beds for flowers and herbs was the cinder block tower that was the compost heap. I added the contents of the bucket to the top and scattered a community of bugs, which—despite being temporarily displaced—would celebrate the arrival of fresh compostables. The compost station was amazing to me for several reasons. First, few people I knew outside our family would consider dinner leftovers as anything but waste to be placed in the garbage can. Second, the critters that the compost pile supported consisted of a who's who of creatures that most people did not want to have around their home, let alone feed them like pets. Third, the sticky, sweet organic material my grandfather would harvest from the compost would render any use of commercially purchased fertilizer unnecessary. My grandfather knew that this was the way to operate a home garden and kitchen—he had been doing it for over a half century!

DID YOU KNOW ?

A typical salad consists of fruits (such as tomato), flowers (such as broccoli), roots (such as carrot), stems (such as celery), seeds (such as sesame), and leaves (such as lettuce)—every plant part!

We rose early every morning to take a walk with my grandfather. He felt it necessary to set the schedule for the day, but my brother and I had it memorized by now. Amazed at the pace of my grandfather, who was sixty years older than us, we figured his health must be connected to all that good, wholesome food that he had eaten his whole life and to his daily activity in the garden. We also knew how much he liked breakfast, and we noted that his steps quickened when we turned the final corner and headed for home. Passing through the quarter-acre garden, he knew there was a melon that was just ripe for picking, and he gave the order for us to find it. It was like a scavenger hunt. We carefully turned over the large leaves, looking for the fruit. Pop had taught us how to determine if a melon was ripe by its color, its smell, and the sound it made when given a gentle knuckle thump. The size of the melon gave this one away without the need of a sniff or a tap. Using the paring knife Pop gave us, my brother cut it from the vine. We proudly brought the prize into the house, and it was promptly sliced for the first course of breakfast.

After breakfast we returned to the garden for some weeding and additional harvesting for lunch and dinner items. My grandfather entrusted us with the tools his father had given him, and I took in the plant maze from the edge of the patio. Planning my task sequence, I balanced my footsteps as I navigated from the trellis where green beans grew to the dense rows of leafy greens. The soil compressed a bit as I knelt down in the soft earth to harvest the remaining radishes from the spring crop. I relished the harvest and paused in the morning sun to smell the sweet soil, feel the bay breeze, and scan the vivid colors of Pop's garden. My brother picked tomatoes of at least three varieties.

Tomatoes on the vine

After a visit to the beach in the early afternoon, we returned home and noticed that the watering can had been placed on the bench near the garden. It was watering time. Though there was a hose that could very easily have delivered water to every part of the garden, Pop preferred to visit each plant with the watering can, and so we did the same.

My grandfather taught me so much about gardens, soil, plants, and cooking. I wrote none of it down at the time, but because I visited a few times a summer for several years during my childhood, I am certain I remember almost everything. The things I do instinctively in my garden today—and many of the garden lessons I teach my own children—have their roots in my grandfather's garden plots. I can still hear his voice when I contemplate a garden activity. My family's home was about an hour's drive inland from the coast, but with the soil being similar to my grandparents' property, I could plant many of the same things, though I never even tried to match the diversity and scale of his garden. This was partly due to the busy schedule of a young boy, but I think mostly it was because Pop's garden, like the man himself, was larger than life.

Pop's hand shovel

Pop's watering can

Because of the lessons provided by my grandfather on gardening and the nature of food, I would go on to other adventures: harvesting huckleberries to be added to morning pancakes (I proudly made these for my grandparents when they would come visit), venturing into the woods to look for hen-of-the-woods mushrooms for a fun addition to an evening meal, and even assisting my father in growing grapes. Today, as an educator, naturalist, father, and active gardener, my approach to soil, plants, pollination, and pest control tends to be more scientific, but the seeds of my love for gardens and all things in a backyard ecosystem were sown in the hours, days, and years spent with my Pop. I have expanded my practices and now plant rain gardens, pollinator gardens, and mushroom gardens in addition to my traditional vegetable plots. Every season brings new ideas, new experiments, and new crops. Though there are failures that occur nearly as often as successes, it is all great fun and a wonderful adventure. On behalf of our ever-growing garden adventure team, I invite you to join us!

See you in the garden!

A garden harvest

GARDEN ACTIVITY

GARDEN FAMILY TREE

It is likely that many of your family members have, or have had, gardens. Make a family tree that includes your relatives and a description and sketch of what they grow (or grew) in their gardens. You can make this an artistic project complete with photos, journal entries, and even recipes from the harvest from your family's gardens!

GARDEN RESOURCES

Garden History—Victory Gardens:

https://www.nps.gov/articles/000/victory-gardens-on-the-world-war-ii-home-front.htm

https://gardens.si.edu/gardens/victory-garden/

CHAPTER 2

HEALTHY GARDENS, HEALTHY PLANET, HEALTHY PEOPLE

Where does our food come from?

I have asked this question of students for many years as part of agriculture, natural resource, and sustainability lessons. The answers that have been given have sometimes been predictable and sometimes surprising: the pantry, the refrigerator, the grocery store, the farmers' market, farms, and even sometimes from nature. Seldom does the response include family or backyard gardens. There was a time not long ago when at least some of the food consumed by a family was grown and harvested right at home. Communities came together to share their bounty and discuss successes and failures in the garden and ideas for improving the harvest. I believe this connection and concern for where food comes from and how it is produced is slowly returning to our families, towns, and global communities.

Many of us experience farms as a landscape feature that we occasionally pass by as we drive from one place to another. The green carpets of single-crop fields can stretch for miles in some parts of the country. Broken only by roads, farmhouses, barns, or other human structures, these farms may give the appearance of verdant landscapes with high levels of productivity to support the humans, many of whom rely almost

DID YOU KNOW ?

About half the land in the United States is used for industrial agriculture.

A barn and silo behind a single-crop field

entirely on these operations for their food. It is true that over the last century, farms as described above have fed an increasing human population here at home and elsewhere around the world. Additionally, big farms are also big businesses, making lots of money for companies that manage the production of everything from coffee to ketchup to ice cream. Much of the farm activity during the last several decades has been described as industrial agriculture.

DID YOU KNOW ?

Although increasing in total acres, only about 1 percent of farmland in the US is under organic production.

Stop for a moment and think about what a plant needs to grow or what a chicken needs to lay an egg. Life in ecosystems across the planet requires some very basic resources to thrive: sunlight, water, and nutrients. Life in a backyard garden or food growing on an industrial farm is no different. The natural processes that support animals and plants in swamps, forests, meadows, and deserts are the very same processes that support the crops and livestock that will become food for people. Insects for pollination, fungi for cycling nutrients, predators to keep populations in check, and trees to provide shade and hold down soil all are essential species for maintaining the health of natural systems. Sometime in the last century or so, people decided that they could try to grow food without nature's support. Unfortunately, this proved to be a mistake.

Basic lessons in the biology of nature will involve the process of photosynthesis. Farmers everywhere work to try to maximize this process. Plants take in carbon dioxide (a gas found in the atmosphere) and use water taken up by the roots of plants in the presence of sunlight to make sugars. It is these products that are then used by plants to make everything from oils and proteins to other molecules that we need in our diet. For farms that raise animals for meat, plants are still needed. Large areas of cropland are used to grow plants that are harvested for feed for chickens, pigs, cows, and other livestock. What are the limits of growing more food? Farmers who want to increase their crops or number of animals simply need more water, more nutrients, and more space. Seems easy, right? The problem is that there are limits to soil nutrients and water in every natural ecosystem. And consider that every farm is found in an area that used to be a grassland or a forest or even a desert.

DID YOU KNOW ?

Farms can produce large amounts of crops even in deserts. Water and nutrients have to be brought to the farm from somewhere else.

INDUSTRIAL AGRICULTURE

As the world's population has grown (now reaching more than eight billion people across the planet), the need to feed all these people has required farming methods that increase crop production, but these approaches come with serious concerns for human and environmental health. Farms have focused on fewer crops (often only one). Humans have pumped more water out of the ground and diverted more water from rivers and lakes. Scientists have invented chemical fertilizers that can boost crop production but also pollute waterways and the atmosphere. Pesticides, chemicals used to kill weeds and insects that reduce crop success, have been spread and sprayed on farms everywhere. Unfortunately, these chemicals have harmed beneficial insects that pollinate the very crops we are trying to grow. Additionally, these chemicals get into streams and rivers and travel through the air to natural habitats and even our neighborhoods where people and wildlife can be harmed. As farms have expanded, natural habitat has been converted to cropland and fields for raising livestock. Lost habitat affects species that keep our natural environment healthy.

But not all hope is lost! Farmers and people everywhere have recognized these problems and have developed some simple solutions. The basic approach? Treat farms as ecosystems, not industries!

Roundup, one of the most commonly used herbicides

WATER

For anyone who has a garden, water is perhaps the most obvious resource needed to keep plants healthy. For most of my life it never occurred to me that water could be limited. For our vegetable and flower gardens at home and at my grandparents' house, there never seemed to be a need to conserve (though my grandfather was always careful with how much he used). On the farms I worked and visited growing up, the irrigation systems always flowed with the water. One doesn't need to go far to realize that water can be in short supply and, more and more, sometimes may not be available in the amount that is required. Farmers and residents alike have taken advantage of some ways to reduce the use of water and still produce food. In and around our homes, there are water conservation practices that we all know to be smart: don't leave the water running, run the washing machine or dishwasher only when full, and irrigate only when needed (I have seen automatic sprinklers come on during rainstorms!).

A second approach focuses on how we bring water to our crops and gardens. A simple solution for reducing water is currently being used by gardeners and farmers alike. Drip irrigation delivers drops of water right to the base of the plants. Water is absorbed by plants mostly through their roots, so irrigating right at ground level is the best way to ensure the plants have enough water. If water ends up on the leaves or adjacent to the planted area, this water is more likely to evaporate (move back into the air).

Water drops on a seedling

Perhaps the most important thing to remember about the needs of your garden plants is that all the required resources are connected. If you have healthy soil in your garden or on the farm, that soil will hold more water! If the soil holds more water, then you will not need to irrigate as much, and the plants have continuous access to moisture.

SOIL

Soil is actually an ecosystem—a defined space in which there are living and nonliving parts that are connected in many ways. So often, people will reference "dirt" as a way to describe the stuff on the ground from which the plants grow. Let us not forget that if the plant is growing from the ground, there must be things in the ground that the plant needs. There are five basic "ingredients" in healthy soil. First, there are minerals: nitrogen, phosphorus, potassium, magnesium, iron, sulfur, and a bunch of other elements from the periodic table (chemistry of life!) that are found as sand, silts, and clays in various combinations.

Soil contains organic material: the remains of leaves, dead bugs, poo from animals, and other materials that are often dark in appearance. This material holds lots of water and can also be a supply of additional nutrients needed by plants and other organisms. Soil contains life! One of the most enjoyable activities for kids in the garden is to use a hand lens to investigate the variety of life in even the smallest sample of soil: worms, pill bugs, millipedes, and other animals, fungi, and bacteria (these are too small to be seen without a microscope) and,

Dark, rich soil to support a young garden plant

of course, plant seeds, roots, and underground stems. All these organisms keep the soil healthy by consuming organic matter, aerating the soil, releasing nutrients, and moving soil around. Soil also contains water. Again, the presence of organic matter will increase the amount of water in the soil. Finally, the space in between soil particles will have gas; the same gases that are found in the air are found (and needed) in the soil. For example, oxygen is available to soil animals and plants in healthy soil. All these things must be present if the soil is to support your garden plants and the crops on a farm.

PESTS

There is no such thing as a pest in nature, but in our gardens and on our farms we identify plants and animals that can reduce our success in growing and harvesting crops. For as long as there has been agriculture, there have been living things that people have tried to keep out of our food plots. Around a hundred years ago, scientists developed new chemical

Japanese beetles

pesticides that were designed to kill the things we do not want on our farms. Homeowners have also taken advantage of these chemicals to treat their yards and home gardens. Though these chemicals have been effective, they have also had unintended consequences.

The most famous case study is that of a chemical known as DDT. This pesticide that came into widespread use in the second half of the twentieth century was used effectively against a whole range of insect species deemed "pests." The problem was that DDT was also harming other species, most notably birds. In her book *Silent Spring*, scientist, environmentalist, and writer Rachel Carson described how bird eggs were weakened by this chemical, and many species were unable to reproduce. Scientists have since realized that other species, including humans, can be affected by this chemical as well.

Avoiding the use of chemicals that kill plant and insect pests may seem difficult, but there are many ways a gardener and farmer can do just that. Most of these methods focus on understanding natural processes. Predators, such as ladybug beetles, can be introduced in order to keep insect pests in check. Mulch or other organic materials that are good for the soil can also be placed at the base of crops to reduce the success of weeds. Remember though: many plants deemed "weeds" are actually beneficial for the garden, and some, such as dandelions, are edible.

Traps can be used to catch insects, and, for small garden plots, problematic insects or weeds can be handpicked. Other natural ways to reduce pest species continue to be developed by universities and state and federal agriculture agencies. In my gardens I have found that by diversifying the plants I grow, no one insect becomes dominant. Focusing on diversifying what you grow can actually increase how much you grow by reducing the success of insects and other pests!

DID YOU KNOW ?

There are more than 10,000 products used around the world that contain chemicals designed to kill pests.

DID YOU KNOW ?

DDT was largely banned in 1972, but soil and water studies even today reveal the long-lasting presence of this chemical.

Dandelion: an edible "weed"

BIODIVERSITY

When farms during the last century were being converted to single-crop landscapes, forest and prairie ecosystems were being replaced with industrial farms that needed large amounts of chemical fertilizers and pesticides and massive irrigation projects to keep them going. At some point we forgot that food ultimately comes from nature and that the best way to produce food is to support natural environments and the organisms that live there. We know this now and have developed more sustainable practices as described above. So much of a farm's or garden's sustainability comes down to the creatures that live there. Want healthy, fertile soil that holds more moisture and supplies needed nutrients? Protect and support soil invertebrates. Want to manage your pests without harsh, dangerous chemicals? Keep natural predators on and near your farm. Essentially, if a farm is a habitat, a home for a diversity of living things, then you will find that the life you support in turn supports your garden or farm. So biodiversity refers not only to what you are growing but also to what you are supporting around the plots where you plant vegetables and flowers. Diversify both, and success is more likely—and a healthy environment is ensured.

Ladybug

Remember that a healthy garden and healthy habitat around your garden also means a healthy you!

FOODSHEDS

I recently ate at a restaurant that described the menu as "farm to table." The server was proud of this fact, and when she introduced herself, she also established that most every ingredient in the meals on the restaurant's menu was obtained from local farms: mushrooms, cheese, grains, chicken, and salad greens. There are many benefits to "eating local." Perhaps the biggest benefit has to do with energy. Think for a moment about how much energy it takes to bring a banana to your breakfast plate. How much energy was needed to plant, grow, harvest, and transport that banana? It's not that we should feel guilty about enjoying food that comes from somewhere else, but we should consider supporting nearby farms and food that is sourced locally whenever possible. A foodshed describes the food produced and available in a given region. Even the most urban of habitats will likely have farms and maybe fisheries not too far away. In southern areas, where the weather may stay moderate in winter, it is possible to enjoy local foods year-round. Even in colder states, we can freeze or can food items when they are fresh to enjoy them when gardens and farms have gone to sleep for the winter. Supporting a foodshed will allow you to invest in your community, and it will save a lot of energy since food does not have to be transported as far or packaged and stored for long periods of time. It will also likely have you getting to know your local food growers if you choose to visit local farms.

Local strawberries

GARDEN ACTIVITY

FOODSHED MAPPING

Task 1: Determine the crops and raw ingredients required to make a breakfast of eggs, toast with butter, blueberries, and orange juice. Using the map below, identify a state where each of the ingredients is likely to be grown. Estimate the distance to your home region.

Task 2: Identify your foodshed. Generally, a 100-mile radius from a single location would constitute a single foodshed, though there are various reasons why this could be smaller or larger.

Identify your location on the map and draw a circle with a radius of 100 miles (200-mile diameter). Identify the different types of food available in your foodshed.

GARDEN RESOURCES

Industrial Farming:
https://www.nrdc.org/stories/industrial-agriculture-101

Sustainable Agriculture:
https://www.nifa.usda.gov/topics/sustainable-agriculture

Small garden, diverse crops

PART TWO

GARDEN ADVENTURES

— CHAPTER 3 —

A GARDEN SLEEPS

One can follow the calendar by observing their garden. The emergence of late-winter weeds, a honeybee sighting, the smell of fresh soil activated by a chilly rain—all these are signposts of the start of the spring garden season. The transfer of indoor seedlings to the raised beds outside, the songs of birds coming in to inspect a nearby shrub or tree, and the evening flashes of fireflies all tell of summer approaching. A garden day cut short by a setting sun, goldenrod blooming, and a passing monarch speak to autumn's arrival. The last harvest of spinach, a frosty coating in the shaded corner of the garden, and the slowed production of eggs from the backyard henhouse all indicate that winter is not far off.

I know people who grow sad at the end of the garden season. The end of fresh veggies and the shorter days and cold nights can leave one longing for the warm, productive days of garden summer. But it is important to keep in mind that, like us, our gardens need a period of rest. Winter may form a cold, hard crust on the ground, limit the activities of wildlife, and present a landscape of bleakness, but your garden is quietly preparing for the promise of next spring!

Under the frozen surface, microbes slow down, but depending on the soil composition and the depth of frost, bacteria and fungi are still making nutrients available for the next growing season. Worms and other invertebrates take shelter in deeper layers or lay eggs for the next generation, ensuring they'll again be ready to go back to work when the moisture and temperature support their activity. You can help your garden sleep and offer additional refuge for soil life by adding layers of compost and leaf litter to your garden plots. Weeds that grow in the late season will help hold down the soil

A winter garden resting

and, as they die back, add additional organic matter to the soil. If you live in a region that gets regular snowfall, a wintry blanket may also help insulate the ground beneath. Plant roots, underground stems, and seeds all have their stored food. Like you, they are waiting for just the right time to emerge in the garden.

DID YOU KNOW ?

Like other organisms, winter temperatures can put some microbes—bacteria and fungi—into a type of "hibernation." Other microbes can still thrive at temperatures well below freezing!

I have just harvested the last of the fruits and vegetables from my garden. It's mid-November and though much of the fall was unseasonably warm, with the promise of an extended harvest, a recent cold snap has set in. A handful of cherry tomatoes, a bouquet of spinach, two green peppers, and a small eggplant made up the final harvest before the last few cold nights have brought the end of the season. I fried the eggplant in olive oil, decorated a homemade pizza with the spinach, and added garlic to the tomatoes and enjoyed the mixture over pasta with a salad that crunched with crisp green peppers. It was now officially time to let the garden rest.

Remaining plants and fruits were cut up to increase the surface area so microbes could break them down in the compost pile. Leaf litter, which had already started

Pizza with spinach

collecting in the beds from the trees in the garden shedding their foliage, was layered over top of the beds. I mixed in some compost for good measure. Leaves in the fall are an essential nutrient source for the soil and for next year's growth.

We enjoy sharing the harvest from our garden. Neighbors, friends, and family are always happy to get a delivery of whatever has been harvested in our small garden plots. As such, I do not preserve as much fresh produce as I would like (though I do freeze huckleberries and blueberries in enough abundance to last into the new year). So, the final meals of November (usually I have some ingredients in our Thanksgiving feast from our garden) are a time to ponder the success and limitations of our harvest. But opening the refrigerator in the winter does still reveal memories and future promise for the garden. Collecting and storing seeds from your harvest is a great way to bring last year's harvest into this year's plantings, and the cool environment of the refrigerator is a good spot to keep seeds during winter. There are different methods to store seeds for different crops, but they all have many of the same tasks in common: separating the seeds, drying the seeds, preparing the seeds, and storing the seeds. There are many resources available to take you step by step through this process.

A chicken inspecting the leaf litter

Walking past the garden beds on my way to the compost in winter, I often remember the green lushness of flowering and fruiting plants of last summer. Knowing that this will be coming again in a couple of months, I am inspired to brave the cold mornings and evenings when I am apt to be delivering the food scraps and meal prep leftovers to our backyard compost heap. Every layer added during the winter represents more nutrients available to enhance the garden soil and provide the slow release of nitrogen, phosphorus, and other elements throughout the growing season.

Harvesting seeds from butternut squash

Winter snow always brings such joy, covering up the garden beds and everything else outside. For our family, a snowstorm is a time of celebration, and we embrace winter activities as we do the pastimes of every other season. Winter rains are a little tougher to take. Cold, rainy days, along with sunset before dinner, can set the stage for a dreary stretch. It is during these times when I am likely to distract myself by browsing the seed options for the spring planting. It is fun to view the options that are available. You can get your seeds from many different sources. I have always had great success with Seeds of Change, because these seeds are harvested from plants grown organically. Try something new! Plant some seeds that you harvested from last year's garden. Always consider the needs of a particular plant, the best planting methods, and the time needed to grow your selected plants. The USDA Hardiness Zone map is an essential resource for the garden planner.

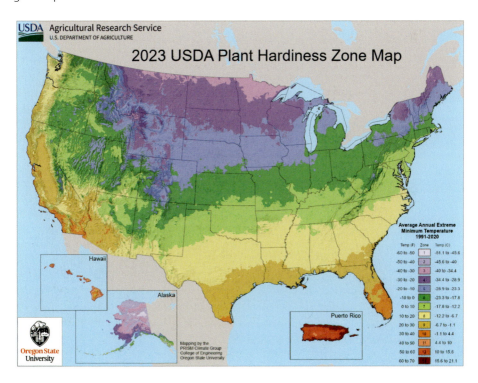

As spring approaches, my family begins to plan for where we will plant our vegetables in our garden. It may seem like a good idea to plant them where they were last year, especially if those plants were producing lots of fruits, flowers, and leaves. Every plant needs certain combinations of nutrients. In addition, some soil organisms may present challenges for your plants, causing disease or reducing their growth. If you plant in the same spot as last year, it may be that those soil organisms will pose a greater problem for that plant and thus reduce your garden success. So, after a season of growing a given plant in a specific plot, it is time to change its location. This is called crop rotation. We have three raised beds and a few other garden plots we plant every season. Three to four years is a common period to bring a crop back to the original location where it was grown before. If you do not have enough space in your garden, maybe try large pots for growing some veggies or perhaps share some plots with a next-door neighbor when rotating your crops.

The days get longer, and an occasional mild day gets you itching for some garden time. Though it may be too early to plant outside, you can do some gardening inside! With a small set of grow lights or a warm, sunny windowsill, you can sow some seeds in containers to get a head start on your growing success! There are many plants you can start indoors. I have found great success with tomatoes, eggplant, melons, cucumbers, and peppers. It's easy to find out if the crops you are interested in growing can be

Paper pot and paper pot roller

started indoors. If using a grow light, adjust the height of the lamps above your seeds. Be sure to plant the seeds at the depth described on the seed packet, and provide enough water to maximize germination. For increased sustainability, consider making your own paper pots with a paper pot roller (available from several seed providers).

Explore these garden-themed adventures to keep gardening in your heart and mind during the winter months. Remember, before you know it, your hands will be in the soil, your seeds will be germinating, and your plans will shift from deciding what to plant to deciding what will be on the menu from your garden.

FROM A YOUNG GARDENER'S JOURNAL: GABRIEL

I enjoy watching the changes in the garden throughout the year. Though winter seems quiet, there is always something interesting in the garden—a bird checking the leaves for food, an occasional insect that wakes up on a warm, late-winter day, or a single spinach leaf that we missed during the fall.

MAPPING YOUR SPRING GARDEN / GARDEN GRID

The grid below represents a garden plot for your backyard or public garden space. Each box represents a 1-by-1-meter raised bed in which you can plant one or more crops/plants. Think about what you like to eat, what you would like to grow, and what others in your family enjoy. Write or sketch in each box on the grid the plant you would like to grow in that space in your garden. Research your selected plants and share your plan with your family and friends.

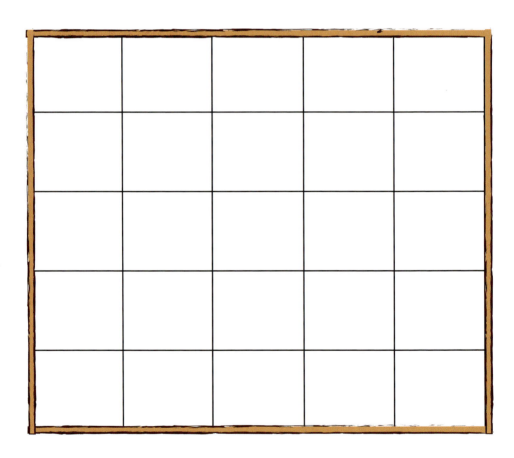

LIST OF PLANTS AND GARDEN NOTES

GARDEN RESOURCES

Planning for Your Spring Garden:

www.cottagefarmstead.com
www.growveg.com
www.seedsofchange.com

— CHAPTER 4 —

A GARDEN AWAKENS

GARDEN NOTES

If March comes in like a lion and out like a lamb, I guess the lion is grumpy for the persistent winter cold, and the lamb takes advantage of all the new shoots of delicious greens that are available in the garden. Though that's not exactly the right interpretation of the saying, it works for me!

Every living thing is adapted to its environment. The interactions of an animal or plant with other species, including feeding activity (who eats whom) and symbiotic relationships (such as a bee and the flower it pollinates), occur in every ecosystem across the planet. In addition, a species of plant or animal is also adapted to the nonliving conditions in its habitat. Temperature, water availability, nutrients, and sunlight all impact a species and its growth and reproduction. Think about any plant or animal and consider its adaptations to the environment. Maybe you will notice its color, shape, movement, or other features that keep that species "happy" in its environment. The vegetables in your garden, whether planted as seeds or seedlings (young plants), are similarly affected both by living and nonliving factors.

When longer days bring more sunlight, it is a signal for gardeners to plan their first outdoor planting. Why do some plants grow well in the cooler days of spring, even if a frost is still possible? Vegetables planted that will flower and then fruit are usually sensitive to the effects of cold temperatures that can damage delicate plant parts. Although leaves may seem delicate, plants will often produce sugars and move them into their leaves to protect from temperatures that approach freezing.

Spring leafies

DID YOU KNOW ?

Salt water will freeze at a lower temperature than fresh water. The same idea protects leafy plants from freezing. More sugar in the leaf means the water will not freeze as readily. Without the added sugar, the leaf would more likely be damaged by temperatures around freezing.

Every seed packet is likely to offer information about when planting is best. The hardiness zones discussed in chapter 3 will be useful for general planning, but the planting details for your selected crop should be reviewed.

Sometimes the feature details of your garden can influence your planting strategy. Stone or brick structures can hold the warmth of the day such that seedlings planted close to such structures may endure those chilly night temperatures a little better than those planted elsewhere. Maintaining a compost-rich soil base will increase the organic content and water-holding capacity. This may allow the ground to absorb more heat during the day. Even slight variation in the elevation of garden plots can also cool differently. Raised beds can be used to keep plants above the cooler, lower areas of the garden. Consider the duration of sunlight that warms the ground. South-facing gardens can take advantage of the early-spring sun for more hours in the day. Fences, shrubs, and garden sheds may also protect from a cold wind. Should you decide to invest more in the warming of your early-spring garden, you can build or install plant covers or netting to protect

Winter grow box

from the cold nights. For the ultimate garden enthusiast, a greenhouse will expand your growing opportunities dramatically!

A little research will reveal the best crops to plant in the early part of the growing season. These include lettuce, spinach, peas, radishes, broccoli, cabbage, turnips, onions, and asparagus. Decide with your family which of these selections (and there are others) would be best, given the preferences and menu items that are favored by kids and adults. Experiment with your planting location and be sure to experiment with your recipes—even brussels sprouts can be prepared to satisfy the most finicky of eaters!

DID YOU KNOW ?

Planting near a single large stone in your garden can create a microclimate: a small area of your garden that can be warmer than other spaces nearby.

GARDEN ADVENTURE

I don't know who was more excited about the first planting, my son or the family chickens.

It was early March when we peeled back the leaf litter and compost that had been layered over the garden beds. The chickens came in quickly, inspecting for earthworms, and they were not disappointed. With recent rain, milder days, and a whole heap of organic matter to work on, the worms were there in full force. We uncovered the adjacent bed so the chickens would be distracted by the invertebrates in that plot, giving us time to examine the soil closely. A few hearty weeds were pulled, and the small field of brown, rich treasure was ours for the planting. Making sure to follow the veggie rotation of our garden plots that we established, we mapped out the beds.

Our preferred leafy greens include mixed lettuce varieties, spinach, and arugula. These cool-weather crops can be sown directly in the ground as seeds. We tied string to two sticks and stretched the line across the bed. Even in a small bed, it can be tricky keeping your seed rows straight! Gabriel used his finger to create a shallow depression

Chickens inspecting a late-winter plot

along the string line. We repeated the process for three more rows, each separated by about a foot. Gabe dropped in one seed at a time every couple of inches along the rows. Once the seeds were planted, we pinched the small soil mounds on either side of the depressions and covered the seeds with soil (about ½ inch or so). Within a few weeks the seedlings would sprout, and we enjoyed fresh salad greens in April, May, and June!

Broccoli was always a tough sell for me as a child. I remember long stretches of time when I was stuck at the dinner table until I finished my steamed broccoli. But now, fresh small crowns of tender broccoli are a welcome addition to salads, and, steamed with some garlic (which you can also grow in your garden), broccoli is a wonderful side dish for many a meal. I even love it on pizza! So now broccoli is a standard crop in our spring and sometimes fall garden. Unlike with the leafy greens that we sow directly in the soil, I start broccoli indoors under grow lights, which are lights suspended above the planted seeds or growing seedlings that allow you to start your spring or summer crops inside.

Gabe with chickens planting spinach and arugula

DID YOU KNOW ?

Adding spinach to a smoothie is a great way to get all the health benefits of this vegetable, especially if it's not a favorite of some people in your family. Plus, it's a great way to use some of your surplus if you have more than you can eat as part of your salad or stir-fry!

Having started our broccoli indoors a few weeks prior, we brought out our seedlings in late March (the calendar will vary by location—again, check your plant hardiness zones). Now the plants were a few inches high with a few leaves on sturdy stems, and we kept them on the outside deck for a few hours at a time in the days before their permanent move to the garden. Called "hardening" the plants, this method provides the plants with a transition from the constant, warm conditions of your home to the variable conditions of outside wind and cooler temperature. This will help the plants grow stronger and likely ensure more success once they're planted in the garden.

Leafy green sprouts from the garden

DID YOU KNOW ?

It is best to use fluorescent or LED lights for your indoor seedlings. They do not put off as much heat and use much less energy than incandescent bulbs.

Our spring garden plan for our plots

The diversity of our early-spring garden offers something for everyone, and though some of the plants will not endure once the temperature climbs, a fall planting of many crops can allow you a second harvest in between the high-summer veggies that thrive in the warmer temperatures.

FROM A YOUNG GARDENER'S JOURNAL: GABRIEL

It is so nice when the weather warms enough to plant the first seeds in our garden. I like growing things inside to start, but my favorite activity in the early spring is planting the spinach seeds directly in the ground.

GARDEN ACTIVITY

WINTER GARDEN SEEDLING RACE

Which leafy green will grow fastest in your late-winter/early-spring garden plots? Find out!

Plant two or three different leafy greens next to each other in the same plot. Document which seeds germinate first and which ones become the first additions to your dinner plate!

GARDEN RESOURCES

Winter Gardening:

https://homesteadingfamily.com/gardening-in-winter-cold-weather-growing-methods/

https://www.motherearthnews.com/organic-gardening/gardening-techniques/winter-gardening-tips-best-crops-zm0z13onzsto/

CHAPTER 5

GARDEN DIVERSITY

GARDEN NOTES

The world needs diversity—on every level. Diverse people, diverse cultures, diverse species . . . and, yes, diverse food! Stroll down the produce aisle at the grocery store, meander the paths of your community garden, or explore the options at a local farmers' market and, inevitably, you will see food that you have never tried before, and sometimes crops that may be completely unfamiliar to you.

Farmers' market

DID YOU KNOW ?

Fewer than a dozen crops provide 75 percent of the calories for the more than eight billion people who live on Earth!

Embracing food diversity has so many benefits. The health value of different plants helps balance the needed nutrients and vitamins in our diets. Our meals can provide us with everything we need if we are sure to embrace the diversity of our food. Growing different crops in the garden helps ensure that a healthy soil base will be able to provide for the unique needs of each plant type. Supporting food diversity also helps increase global food security. History has shown that depending on only one crop in a region can be risky, because disease or weather events may result in a major failure of a single crop.

Cucamelons

Remember that diversity benefits in your garden extend to the other species that are found in the yard. The flowers of your fruits and vegetables will appeal to a greater diversity of pollinators, and increasing the plants in your nonfood garden habitats—shrubs, trees, and flowers—will also help ensure a balanced garden ecosystem.

We were always told as children to "eat a rainbow." If the fruits and vegetables that we eat reveal a diversity of pigments, it is likely that this diet is providing us with a balance of nutrients and a variety of human health benefits.

Bee on a cucumber flower

Eating a rainbow

Exploring food options allows us to connect with different cultures and people. It is very likely that right in your neighborhood there are families growing food that has come from their personal histories and regions of origin. A neighbor of mine who grows bitter melons shared not only his harvest but also recipes that connected me to his family, his country of origin, and his traditions.

Many gardeners start their garden adventure with some of the common fruits and vegetables; tomatoes, cucumbers, and peppers all are frequent favorites. And, surely, we have recipes that might require that more area in our plots be planted with those items. For example, I have friends who love to make pesto and include basil in much of their cooking. Since it is easy to grow, many of their garden pots and plots are used for growing this specific herb. Embrace your favorites and start simple, but keep in mind that increasing the diversity of your plot will likely enhance your knowledge and the enjoyment of growing your own food.

Bitter melon

It was pizza night, a Friday night tradition in our home started by my father over thirty years ago. This tradition features homemade dough, fresh herbs from the garden, and, often, an experiment in toppings. We have hosted extended family, neighbors, close friends, and visitors from out of town for pizza night. Though I admit I make a mean pie (thin dough with the herbs mixed in with the flour before rising is the secret), the tradition belongs to the entire family. We have planned and unplanned competitions for the best pizza, and I have relied heavily on the diversity of my garden for event-winning

Tomato harvest

combinations. It is during the warmer months that some of the greatest creations have been born. This time of year, not only can we take advantage of gifts from the garden, but we often eat there as well. When dining alfresco, we can actually smell the herbs baked into the crust while we sit next to the beds that have next week's harvest. Topping selections can be a shared event; while swapping stories between the garden beds, we make predictions about the tastiest pie for the evening.

As we go strolling into the garden, the ingredient options can be sampled as they are considered. There are some predictable constants among the topping selection, since it is hard to beat a pizza with fresh basil and rosemary. The tomato diversity is often celebrated. Yellow pear tomatoes, chocolate cherry tomatoes, heirloom varieties, and classic Roma tomatoes can be selected for a solo topping or brought together to make for a magical combination. Broccoli, arugula, zucchini squash, and eggplant all add color, texture, and flavor to the meal. Ground cherries, a type of husk tomato, produce small fruits hidden within a papery lantern-like covering and are a special treat that always add some sweet interest to the toppings we have used over the years. These tasty delights I acquire from a friend whose backyard garden is several times the size of my own. However, this tasty little gem is on the short list of species to be planted in my backyard in the future.

All the options described above can be comple-mented with some oyster or wine cap mushrooms (a fun adventure worthy of their own chapter, so read on!). By far, the pizza that has gone down in family lore is a simple combination of fig, rosemary, and hot peppers. The pepper and rosemary plants we grow from seed, as is true of most of the "croppings" (seems appropriate to combine "crops" and "toppings" when we are talking pizza, no?). But our fig tree is worthy of individual attention, and the story of how it came to be in our garden is as fun as the pizzas that are adorned with these sweet fruits.

Ground cherry

Many years ago, my grandfather traveled to the village on the island of Sicily from which his grandparents emigrated. He was embraced by cousins he did not even know, and the entire town celebrated the visit of an American relative over the course of a few days. As a parting gift, he was given a large burlap bag of figs. With only forty-eight hours left on the trip, my grandfather refused to let a single fig go to waste, and he ate them with every meal until—hours before his return flight—he finished the last few. Though details have always been left to the imagination of those who would hear the story, his eight-hour plane ride home proved to be a significant gastrointestinal challenge—though this never stopped him from sharing the details of his wonderful stop in the mountains of his ancestral home.

Figs from our family tree

Once my grandfather was back home, my father ordered him a small plant of the same fig variety that he had enjoyed while visiting Italy. That plant would eventually be transplanted twice: first from my grandfather's garden to my father's and then to my backyard, where it now produces an ample crop each year. This is just an example of how embracing diversity in your garden connects us to people, places, and experiences, and I know that you too will accumulate memories and moments that will become part of your family's story.

Our pizza nights have always been a celebration. A combination of gardens, recipes, food experiments gone right (and wrong), and shared meals with those who are close to us. Celebrating garden diversity extends beyond the food put on the table. We have explored techniques of growing different crops together, and each year we are able to grow more on the same-sized plots as the season before. In the small raised beds of our symmetrical garden plots, we have married an increase in total harvest with the diversification of options for our pizza, for our salads and for meals that we have yet to prepare!

Intercropping: planting different crops together

FROM A YOUNG GARDENER'S JOURNAL: GABRIEL

I have tried many new things from our garden. Probably one of my favorite memories was eating the flowers of our zucchini squash. I checked to make sure there were no bugs inside the flower, then brought it in as a decoration for our dinner plate. I didn't know you could eat them. Probably the prettiest thing I ever ate!

GARDEN ACTIVITY

THE GLOBAL GARDEN

Take a walk through the produce section your local grocery store and look up where in the world each of the fruits and vegetables comes from. How many countries are on your list?

GARDEN RESOURCES

Diversity in the Garden:

https://www.croptrust.org *(Crop Trust is an organization that focuses on protecting crop diversity and increasing the availability of diverse crops to the world.)*

https://www.foodunfolded.com/discover/category/food-around-the-world *(Explore food from around the world.)*

CHAPTER 6

BACKYARD CHICKENS

GARDEN NOTES

Over the past couple of years, the fluctuation in egg prices seems to have brought about an increase in the interest in owning backyard chickens. Many homeowners have embarked on the journey to host their own flock right in the backyard. With a moderate amount of space and some training, along with an initial investment in the coop, nesting space, and food and water container, starting a flock of backyard chickens can truly be a fun adventure that brings enjoyment, entertainment, and a steady supply of delicious eggs to your table.

Domestic chickens are thought to have originated in Southeast Asia thousands of years ago. Descendants from wild fowl species in the same area, domestic chickens spread quickly to other regions. Though initially they were not a major food source in all communities, chickens were easy to transport, keep, and feed, and they provided a ready supply of eggs and meat. They were destined to become a valued addition to farms and gardens.

DID YOU KNOW ?

Around the globe, there are as many as a hundred recognized breeds of chicken.

Up close with Agnes, one of our chickens

Chickens are now found the world over, and many breeds are raised for egg production, meat, or both. Each breed is adapted to specific environmental conditions, and the diversity of size, color, and features is surprisingly large. Just like with garden vegetables, some varieties are quite rare, and, as with other food species, there are organizations that promote the protection of rare breeds. This effort is led by organizations such as the Livestock Conservancy, with the stated purpose to "protect endangered livestock and poultry breeds from extinction." As is true of every species in nature, having a diversity of breeds helps ensure the future of life in our farm ecosystems and, in turn, the future of food security.

In many breeds of chicken, the formation of eggs occurs amazingly fast (every backyard chicken owner is surely amazed by the productivity of their chickens). Some breeds can lay more than three hundred eggs per year per hen! For fertilized eggs produced on farms or in gardens with hens and roosters, hatching will occur in a matter of weeks. Chicks will grow quickly into pullets (young chickens). It will typically take a few months for young chickens to mature and start laying eggs of their own. The exact timing of the onset of egg laying will depend on the breed, nutrition, housing, and light levels.

Though chickens have been domesticated for thousands of years, in many places agricultural interest in maintaining large flocks of chickens is relatively recent. In the 1800s and early 1900s here in the US, the use of chickens for eggs and poultry was typically

DID YOU KNOW ?

Just like in wild species, some domestic chicken breeds are endangered. Examples include the Burmese Bantam and the Scots Dumpy.

The Scots Dumpy, an endangered breed of chicken

Chicken mayhem

a local business, often via small-scale, family farms. From the early 1900s into the middle part of the last century, interest increased and, as the environmental factors affecting egg production and the biology of egg laying were better understood, serious attention was given to egg and meat production from chickens on a larger scale. It is interesting that backyard and small-farm chicken flocks were the norm when my grandfather was young, and now we are seeing a resurgence of the interest in housing chickens in our gardens and backyards!

Today, not only are chickens kept for egg laying and the health benefits of locally produced protein that complements the various other food items in our gardens, but they have also become celebrated additions to the biodiversity of our homes and neighborhoods. Backyard chickens provide healthful food, enjoyment, and aesthetic appeal—enriching our lives with their presence in sometimes surprising ways!

GARDEN ADVENTURE

It was a beautiful early-spring morning. A mild overnight temperature allowed us to keep our windows open to enjoy the fresh air and the promise of the approaching garden season. I took a deep breath as the rays of sunlight entered the kitchen. The air was fresh, cool, and moist as it filled my lungs. Right on cue, another sensory experience brought an immediate smile to my face. Cackles, clucks, and squawks from the garden signaled the start to the day. I find it amusing that we are not allowed to keep roosters in our town because of the noise they make around daybreak. Apparently, no one told my small flock of hens that a noisy morning was not allowed.

The chickens were celebrating the new day just as I was, albeit in a slightly more raucous fashion. I couldn't help but let out a chuckle of my own, since I knew the neighbors must also be taking in the sounds of our small backyard farm . . . and that some of them may not have been enjoying the wake-up call as much as I was. For the most part, however, our small, quiet street was enhanced by our chickens; many neighbors were thrilled to receive the occasional delivery of surplus eggs.

A neighbor of mine can see our garden from his backyard. He likes the diversity of activities that go on in our outdoor space. He enjoys, in particular, the antics of our small flock of chickens. Scratching, cackling, pecking, and perching, our chickens are often on full display for any observer curious enough to locate the hens seeking out their favorite spot in the garden. On a couple of occasions, a wayward bird has wandered beyond the cedar fencing of our backyard and has gone poking around the flower beds and shrubs in my neighbor's yard. After an initial span of amusement, he comes around to inform us of the escapee and helps us direct her so she can rejoin the flock. Though he has graciously accepted a variety of our homegrown fruits and vegetables from the garden, he is vehement about not accepting eggs.

The flock

Hens in the nesting box

Chickens on duty

I attempted to uncover the reason for his resistance but could not really conclude anything other than that he finds it uncomfortable to eat the eggs from the birds that he observes. Was it their color? The fact that he could observe them poop? The things he observed them eating (insects and other garden invertebrates)? In the end, every chicken forms and lays an egg the same way. The nutrients found in eggs (and all of our food) must come from the soil, the water, the air, and the plants and animals that are part of the garden or farm ecosystem. The chickens in our garden have the best of everything: pesticide-free food, space to exercise and forage for insects, fresh water, and a clean roost site where they can rest and have ready access to the nesting box where they lay.

Our chickens are hyline browns. Much like the brownish-red color of their plumage, the eggs they lay are light brown. Our friend, who grew up and spent most of his life in the city, referenced that the eggs he ate were always white. Our eggs seemed unfamiliar.

Perhaps the habits of food shopping and the recognition of what is "normal" were also affecting his thoughts about our eggs. Despite my insisting that he will not enjoy a tastier, fresher egg than those that we have offered, he remains settled on his opinion. I find this a curious position and can't help but conclude that this example represents a disconnect between people and the living creatures that ultimately provide us with sustenance.

Several years ago when our town passed an ordinance to allow small backyard chicken flocks (I was an active promoter of this movement), I rushed up to the town hall to make sure that I would secure one of the twenty-five permits that were to be issued for our backyard chicken pilot program. My family teased me about my insistence that we needed to hurry into town so we wouldn't be without a permit for the program. I had promoted with enthusiasm the idea of having backyard chickens over the past year, and my effort resulted in permit #6. In the end, there was no need to rush—only about half of the available permits were claimed by families in town. Still, I was thrilled to be one of the pioneers, and I signed up for the required training and made arrangements to pick up our new residents for our garden.

DID YOU KNOW ?

There are thousands of backyard chickens in every city across the country.

DID YOU KNOW ?

The color of a chicken's earlobe is a good indicator of the color of the egg that it will lay.

Eggs in a diverse range of sizes and colors

I had done quite a bit of reading on keeping backyard chickens and spoke at length with the farm staff where we would purchase our birds. After the construction of our coop and nesting box, we were ready to pick up our birds. We drove to Far Wind Farm and picked up our young hens.

After a period of several days of keeping the chickens in their new coop so they would connect with their home roost, we gradually allowed them to explore the garden. Everyone in our family was knowledgeable about the care of our chickens and the working

—> 2024 <—
MERCHANTVILLE
CHICKEN LICENSE
#3

Our chicken permit

of the coop. Still, we had much to learn. In the early days of caring for the flock, I became a bit too confident in their daily patterns. One evening I waited too long to confirm their return to the coop and found two of the chickens roosted in the walnut tree above our house. Unable to retrieve them, I woke up early the next morning to offer them a special treat of melon, which they immediately descended from their overnight perch to enjoy.

I have since become vigilant about the nightly timing of closing the run and coop.

We were also overly optimistic about the chickens meeting our two dogs. Both canines were elderly gentlemen, but we found out that nothing brings out the vim and vigor of an older dog like a tempting flock of hens. Though there was an initial close call (let's just say one of our dogs got a mouthful of feathers), all the chickens were fine after an initial emotional scare. We also found the chickens most ambitious when it came to exploring the gardens. We have had to balance the location of our plants, both flowers and veggies, with the range of our chickens when they are roaming free.

Reny, looking at the chickens

A resting chicken

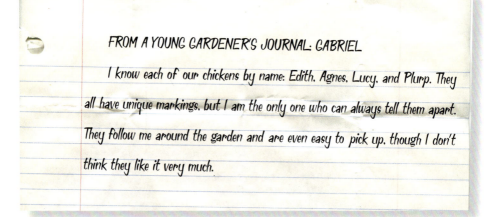

FROM A YOUNG GARDENER'S JOURNAL: GABRIEL

I know each of our chickens by name: Edith, Agnes, Lucy, and Plurp. They all have unique markings, but I am the only one who can always tell them apart. They follow me around the garden and are even easy to pick up, though I don't think they like it very much.

Though it is now largely my son and I who care for the chickens, the learning process continues and our family immensely enjoys having the flock enhance our garden. We have shared our egg bounty and chicken experiences with family, friends, and neighbors. Membership in the community backyard chicken guild has increased, and we often share stories and tips on care and maintenance. Despite the enthusiasm of receiving fresh eggs from our backyard birds, to my knowledge we have not recruited any new backyard chicken practitioners among our family—but we are now lifelong backyard chicken enthusiasts!

GARDEN ACTIVITY

BACKYARD CHICKEN BUDGET

Keeping a flock of backyard chickens is an investment of time, effort, and money. Balancing your budget and your time is really important when it comes to evaluating the pros and cons of maintaining a backyard flock.

Here are some data for your consideration:

Data: Our family spends 20 minutes a day, on average, tending to the needs of the chickens, harvesting eggs, and maintaining the coop.

Analysis: How much time will you spend per week? Per month? Per year? Discuss with your family members who will participate. Who will do each task?

A dozen eggs from our chickens

Data: We buy organic pellets for our chickens. Each 40-pound bag lasts about 25 days and costs about $27 (we have four chickens).

Analysis: For a given year, calculate the pounds of feed you will need, the number of bags you will purchase, and the total cost of the food.

Data: Our four chickens give us, on average, 3 eggs a day. At the writing of this chapter, a dozen organic eggs cost about $6.00.

Analysis: Calculate the number of eggs produced per year. Determine the number of dozens that are yielded. How much are these eggs worth?

Now balance your budget. Does keeping the backyard chickens save you money? Does it cost you more than the eggs are worth? Discuss the financial pros and cons with your family.

GARDEN RESOURCES

Backyard Chickens:
https://www.mypetchicken.com/
https://www.petmd.com/bird/backyard-chickens-101-raising-chickens-beginners

CHAPTER 7

BERRY RAMBLE

GARDEN NOTES

This spring we are planting a few blueberry shrubs in our garden. The rich, compost-based soil in our garden supports a variety of crops. Blueberries grow well in sandy, well-drained soils that have organic matter to provide nutrients but also have a different chemistry from what many crops require. One of the most important soil factors is the pH, a measure of the soil's acidity.

DID YOU KNOW ?

The pH scale ranges from 0 to 14. Values under 7 are acidic; the lower the number, the more acidic the soil. Many crops grow well between 6 and 8, but blueberries, cranberries, and huckleberries grow well with a pH from 4 to 5.

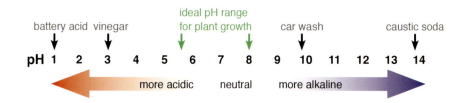

Only 20 miles east from our home is the self-proclaimed blueberry capital of the world, Hammonton, New Jersey. The soils of the Pine Barrens are naturally acidic; consequently, berry farming works well throughout the million acres of the Pine Barrens. Elsewhere, like my backyard, the soil must be adjusted to support the blueberry shrubs.

Some of my early memories of berry picking had me in the undergrowth of the forests near my home. Though blueberry farms were all over the region where I grew up, wild berries were plentiful in the natural habitats of the Pine Barrens. Nature's garden provided several types of berries that we harvested: blueberries, cranberries, and

Blueberry bush

huckleberries. Each plant in the wild has its own specific habitat. Black huckleberries and lowbush blueberries are found abundantly as low shrubs in the upland pine and oak forests with sandy, sometimes dry soil beneath. Highbush blueberries thrive in the wet thickets and swampy woods of wetland habitats. Cranberries are found right along the margin of boggy habitats and can often be temporarily covered by water after heavy rains fill rivers and lakes.

My love of berry picking as a child also led me to an early business enterprise. Selling containers of wild berries at the end of my driveway did result in a modest income; I could sell a pint of wild huckleberries for two dollars (not bad for 1982!). I suppose if I had evaluated my income on a per hour basis, I would have abandoned my picking. It is likely that my parents may have placed a strategic phone call to some of their friends in the neighborhood so as to keep me at my berry stand.

As I think about it, it's amazing I had any surplus to sell. The number of berries that made it into the collection bucket was probably less than half the number that I picked. The telltale signs of my foraging habits were worn on my face and clothes. Purple smudges and stains could not be chalked up merely to picking and drop-ping berries in the bucket. My mom would question the bounty I would bring home, wondering why it took so long to fill a small container. She and I both knew the reason why, and a guilty plea was never required.

Though I was never one to follow recipes as a child (on more than one occasion, an attempt at baking treats for a school fundraiser would be a colossal failure), it seemed pretty straightforward to me that adding fresh berries to any dish seemed like a good idea. Other people embraced my baking philosophy and enjoyed the muffins, bread, cakes, and pies I made. How can you go wrong with flour, sugar, and berries?

DID YOU KNOW ?

Not every fruit that is called a berry is actually a berry! Blueberries, huckleberries, and cranberries all are true berries. But strawberries and blackberries are not true berries!

Cranberry plant

Wild berries

One of my favorite places to pick berries are the fields at Whitesbog, New Jersey. The site, found within a state forest and home to one of the regional offices of the Nature Conservancy, is the place where the cultivated blueberry was developed in the early 1900s as part of a collaborative project between scientists from the USDA and Elizabeth White, an early pioneer of blueberry research and a family member of the Whitesbog Cranberry Farm. There was some question whether the wild blueberries of New Jersey's Pine Barrens could be cultivated as a commercial crop. Elizabeth White had a clever plan. Enlisting the help of

Elizabeth White's
berry gauge

community members from throughout the region, she distributed gauges that had holes that would allow small fruit to drop through, but larger berries would not pass. These larger berries were then kept, and the shrubs from which they came were dug up and transplanted to the experimental plots at the family farm. Crossing selected plants, White and her partners would produce larger and larger berries until a crop of plants could produce berries with consistent taste and size.

The full story of Elizabeth White can be found here: https://nj.gov/state/historical/assets/pdf/it-happened-here/ihhnj-er-blueberries.pdf

It is a special experience to pick berries from the remnant fields still holding fruit at Whitesbog. The cranberry operation there continues, but those who know of the history of blueberry farming are lucky to be able to harvest and enjoy blueberries from some of the first fields that brought commercial berries to the market.

GARDEN ADVENTURE

I had decided that this was the spring and summer for a berry tour of visiting neighbors, farms, and wild sites where berries were growing. A friend of mine in Medford, New Jersey, was hoping to increase the harvest in the family's back gardens, and I came to visit to help with a plant inventory. Like so many residents who live on the edge of the Pine Barrens, my friend needed to achieve a delicate balance in order to grow the desired variety of crops.

Raised beds near the house were designated for growing leafy greens, cucumbers, and tomatoes. Built a couple of feet off the ground, this would help keep bunnies and other small creatures from browsing the veggies—but keeping deer and groundhogs away from the plants is an ever-present challenge. Having decided to maximize native plants, sedges, teaberry, native mosses, and lichens provided a verdant patchwork of groundcover in the backyard. It looked as though a garden gnome might scramble from one island of vegetation to another. The back of the property sloped down toward some swampy woods, and right along the boundary between the drier soil and wetland, highbush blueberry shrubs branched from the ground. Growing to heights of more than 10 feet, the branches hung heavy with dark blue berries on this late June day.

Ready to pick!

Highbush blueberry

I wasn't the only one to take notice. The robins gathered nearby, and a catbird called from the wet thicket beyond the garden. It seemed that there were plenty of blueberries to share, but a diverse community of birds and other species can make surprisingly quick work of a blueberry feast. Discussing how to keep the birds from eating the ripe berries with my friend, I mentioned the one method that seems to work the best. Though the effort required may be significant, adding a wooden frame over the bushes with some light netting can keep the fruit safe. If the frames are built with locking hinges and if the netting is carefully rolled after the season, the construction effort can be useful for several years. After briefly considering the effort and investment, as well as contemplating

DID YOU KNOW ?

Planting berry shrubs in your garden not only supplies a delicious harvest for your family but also can be a key habitat enhancement to support backyard wildlife—assuming you are willing to share!

Catbird

the joy of watching backyard birds supported by blueberries growing wild in the garden, my friend settled on the idea of sharing the bounty with nature. I agreed.

When Father's Day came, my selection of a family activity focused on the availability of blueberries at our favorite organic farm, Fred Plus Three. Having been managed for several decades by a retired school teacher, the farm is now managed by his family members and offers pick-your-own experi-

ences at their two farm plots. Unlike some of the more commercial pick-your-own businesses, this farm has no gift shop, no wagon rides, and no petting zoo. Instead, this farm has an old pickup truck where you can borrow a half-gallon metal bucket with a thick string to tie around your waist for picking. Sandy trails with hand-painted

signs indicate the fields that are open for picking. We walked through the high grass and clover patches, which supported a noticeable diversity of invertebrates, as we made our way out to the field with ripe berries. Even at a distance, the blue of the berries contrasted with the bright green of the leaves, and the hanging branches provided evidence for the abundance of fruit.

The berries plunked into the metal can, sometimes two or three at a time, and it didn't take us long to collect four large cans of berries. Having been a professional picker as a teenager, I tied twin cans to my waist and was able to fill both during our hourlong harvest.

No matter how many berries we pick—and we usually harvest about three times a year—we rarely have frozen berries beyond the end of the

Luna with berries

year. There are so many uses for them, including for fruit smoothies, oatmeal toppings, homemade blueberry ice cream, pie, muffins, pancakes, and—my very favorite—blueberry buckle. Beyond our own recipes and meals—and we can find a way to use blueberries at any time of day and with almost any meal—we also enjoy sharing our bounty. Even the grumpiest of neighbors and the most trying day can be turned around when you share handpicked berries with a friend.

Though not every fruit with "berry" in its name is actually a berry, there is great joy in picking other berries as well. Blackberries and raspberries can grow abundantly, even in the most neglected of gardens. It is always a joyous occasion—and a mandatory break is required—when, on a summer hike, we come across some blackberries or raspberries in season. We recently harvested some mulberries from a neighbor's yard and made a delicious mulberry lemon bread that we shared with neighbors and friends. Other berry fruits are to be found throughout the neighborhood. Strawberries and raspberries are traded for eggs, spinach, and mushrooms: the beauty of a community garden shared harvest!

Raspberries

Bowl of berries

MY FAVORITE BLUEBERRY RECIPE:

Blueberry Buckle

Mix 1 cup sugar and a 1/2 cup of butter till smooth.

Add 2 eggs, 1 at a time, and mix.

Add 3 1/2 cups of flour, 2 tablespoons of baking powder, and a pinch of salt and mix.

Carefully add 3 1/2 cups of berries and gently fold batter till berries are distributed throughout.

Bake in a preheated oven at 370 F for 45 minutes or until a utensil is inserted and comes out clean.

Visits to farms and gardens are wonderful for the opportunity to spend time with friends and harvest a predictable yield of delicious berries. But I must say that some of my favorite memories of berry rambles are from the woodland and thicket explorations that offered a yield of both fruit and magic. A streamside hike in one of your favorite natural places may result in you coming upon a blueberry stand. Thick, gray, lichen-clad stems that support branches with delicious blueberries can offer a snack, a photo opportunity, wildlife watching, or a peaceful moment of awe-inspired fascination with the colors, shapes, and textures of nature that delight the nature enthusiast.

Huckleberries in flower

I recently returned to the woods near my childhood home. Walking with my son, we passed stretches of habitat that had been converted to manicured lawns and perfectly defined mulch beds, devoid of any native plantings. The occasional pitch pine, lower branches having been neatly trimmed, gave the only evidence of the natural forest that had been here thirty years ago. I imagined the presence of thick stands of black huckleberry bushes that produced the fruit I had sold at my roadside table when I was his age. I paused, sad for this small piece of lost nature, but looked forward to our next exploration that could bring us to a habitat where bunches of berries would be waiting to be picked.

FROM A YOUNG GARDENER'S JOURNAL: LUNA

I don't know what I liked more: picking the berries or eating them. There were so many growing on the same bush. I could have just kept on picking!

Wild berries near my childhood home

FROM FLOWERS TO FRUITS

Fruits form when flowers are pollinated. Many fruits require insect pollinators. Observe in your garden the pollinators that visit flowers of a specific plant. You can observe tomatoes, cucumbers, or blueberries. Mark a specific flower, or a group of flowers, by tying a light, short, colored thread beneath the flower on the stem. Follow the process of pollination.

Who visits the flower? How many times? How long does it take to go from flower to fruit?

Try to observe a group of flowers on a given branch or stem. How many of them develop into fruits?

GARDEN RESOURCES

The Health Benefits of Blueberries:

https://www.webmd.com/diet/health-benefits-blueberries

Planning and Planting Your Berry Garden:

https://www.thehiphomestead.com/how-to-design-a-berry-walk-garden/

Our favorite blueberry farm

CHAPTER 8

DON'T FEAR THE FUNGI

GARDEN NOTES

My adventures in mushroom growing are rather recent. In 2020, many of us had a lot more time on our hands to explore new projects on the home front. It was then that I took a renewed interest in fungi and how they could be part of my garden adventures. Thinking back to my younger years, I find myself surprised that it took so long to rekindle a love for mushrooms. Growing up in the Pine Barrens of New Jersey, I had ample opportunity to explore the woodlands and wetlands in search of interesting creatures. Though I delighted in seeing reptiles and amphibians and came to identify bird calls readily, I also found fascination in the world of mushrooms. A kindly neighbor, Mrs. Jenkins, served as my first fungal tour guide (she was an amazing naturalist who taught me a great deal about the Pine Barrens). Her love for fungi was infectious. Always with a woven basket under one arm, she would delight at the sight of boletes and morels; though she collected select samples for her meals, she always spent the time to admire the fungi before she would add them to her harvest. I confess I knew much more about wild mushrooms as a child from my walks with Mrs. Jenkins than I do even to this day.

Author's Note: Never eat a mushroom from the wild unless you are 100 percent certain that it is an edible species and that a knowledgeable and trusted adult is on hand to confirm the identification.

Wild mushroom: bolete

With confirmation from my parents that Mrs. Jenkins was indeed knowledgeable about edible species, I trusted her identifications and enthusiastically tried many samples from the options that she offered me.

As a teenager I would travel with my uncle right before the holidays to the mushroom farms of southeastern

Pennsylvania. The self-proclaimed "mushroom capital of the United States" is Kennett Square, Pennsylvania. The title is likely deserving, since about half of the country's mushrooms are produced here. We would travel the hour and a half from home and buy dozens of wooden baskets of button mushrooms. Once back home, we would decorate the baskets and deliver unique holiday gifts to friends and family.

Years later, after my first few years teaching, I decided to go back to school for my master's degree. A part-time student, I sometimes had to take the classes that were offered in the evening, and one semester my only choice was Fungal Ecology. My initial worry was that the three-hour class on a Monday night might prove too much for a part-time student, but within the first half hour of the first class, I was captivated, yet again, by fungi. To this day, this was one of the most amazing classes I ever took, and fungi ended up being the focus of my graduate research project.

Fungi are so much more than the mushrooms that seem to pop up overnight in gardens and woodlands. Hidden within the soil, their extensive network of filaments, called mycelia, performs a variety of roles in ecosystems. They break down dead matter, they form bridges between neighboring trees, they help build soil, they feed many other organisms, and, in fact, they even prey upon some species of soil invertebrates!

Mushrooms and mycelia below the soil

Mushrooms prepared for an omelet

DID YOU KNOW ?

Mycorrhizal fungi link up with the roots of plants to increase the surface area for absorbing water and nutrients. More than 90 percent of plants have these fungal partners!

GARDEN ADVENTURE

It would be possible to fill my entire garden journal just with notes on fungi. They play multiple roles in your garden, and their diversity and function can be observed in surprising places. So often unnoticed and underappreciated, fungi are a diverse assemblage of species that are so different from other organisms that they occupy their own kingdom of life on our planet. From your compost pile, to an old tree stump, to the surfaces of leaves on the plants in your garden, fungi are everywhere!

DID YOU KNOW ?

There are over 100,000 species of fungi on our planet!

Some of the diverse types of fungi found in nature are shown above and on the next two pages.

During the spring, one of my favorite early garden activities is to transfer the rich, organic material from my compost onto the raised beds that will soon support this year's harvest of fruits and vegetables. When you're lifting a mound of compost from the heap, a closer inspection will reveal a network of white filaments threading through the soil. This mesh of living fibers is the mycelium of the fungi. Our familiarity with mushrooms may lead some to assume that they are observing the main part of the fungi. In reality, the mycelia represent the bulk of biomass of many species.

The mycelium functions to break down organic matter, decomposing material into valuable nutrients. In types of fungi that work with plants to increase the absorptive surface area of the roots, the mycelia physically link up with (and sometimes grow into) the root structures. Predatory fungi will make loops of their mycelia in order to trap worms in the soil. The mushrooms that emerge from the ground, or from woody substrates in the garden, also grow from the mycelia. Additionally, many species obtain nutrition from eating fungi; these species include small mammals, some birds, turtles, and a wide variety of invertebrates.

Mycelia

Box turtle—a fungivore!

As many beneficial roles as fungi play in our gardens and in nature, they can also present challenges to the gardener. There are a variety of fungal diseases that infect various plant parts and hinder the growth of plants or reduce the quality of the harvest. One of the common fungal diseases I contend with in the garden is tomato anthracnose, a fungal disease that causes dark, sunken patches on the surface of tomatoes.

Anthracnose fungi can also affect other plants and other plant parts. Like with other fungal diseases, excess moisture can increase the incidence of anthracnose, so proper soil drainage and removing diseased portions of plants can help address these problematic fungi.

With so much emphasis on the roles of fungi in benefiting or harming the plants in your garden, it may be easy to forget that fungi themselves can be a crop! I have delighted in growing fungi over the past few years and am now an enthusiastic, though novice, farmer of fungi. I ordered my mushrooms from North Spore, a company in Maine that specializes in providing mushrooms, supplies, and wonderful educational resources. We have grown a few species: wine caps, oyster mushrooms, and shiitakes.

Each grows best with a specific substrate, and most species thrive when kept out of direct sunlight and under humid conditions. The process of "planting" your fungi involves introducing the mushroom spawn (mycelium of the fungal species plus the substrate on which it grows) to the organic material where it will thrive. Each spring we grow oyster mushrooms in prepared straw baskets and wine caps on hardwood mulch beds. This year we are growing shiitake mushrooms on oak logs. The method that introduces the spawn to the substrate is called inoculation, and how this is done differs from species to species and from one substrate to another. If this seems like a lot of difficult details, it is not! With a little bit of knowhow and careful management of your fungi, you will be enjoying the delicious bounty of your fungal gardens.

Anthracnose on a fruit

Bags of spawn

Mushroom spawn up close

Prepping the substrate

Oyster mushroom flush

Oyster mushroom—countertop flush

DID YOU KNOW ?

You can order a self-contained mushroom box that allows you to grow mushrooms right on your countertop! We have been enjoying golden oyster mushrooms in late winter before much of our outdoor gardening is underway. They are a delightful addition as a pizza topping or an omelet ingredient!

Consider expanding the presence of fungi in your garden. They will quietly support the ecology of your vegetable plots and your compost pile through decomposition and food web interactions. Some of the sites in your garden that may not be suitable for growing plants might be just the perfect spot for growing edible fungi. We have found this to be an amazing addition to our garden adventures, and—so long as you don't fear the fungi—you will too!

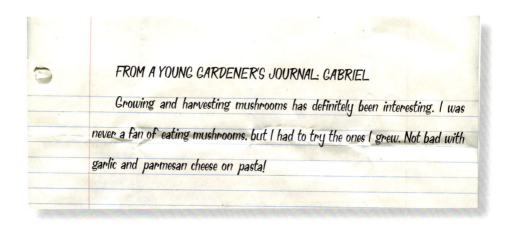

FROM A YOUNG GARDENER'S JOURNAL: GABRIEL

Growing and harvesting mushrooms has definitely been interesting. I was never a fan of eating mushrooms, but I had to try the ones I grew. Not bad with garlic and parmesan cheese on pasta!

FINDING FUNGI AND MUSHROOM MAPPING

Spend some time in your garden searching for fungi. Make a map of your garden and mark the spots where you find fungi. How many different species? Are you seeing mycelia or the fruiting bodies (mushrooms)? What are they growing in or on? What do the sites where fungi are found share in common?

GARDEN RESOURCES

North Spore:

> https://www.northspore.com *(a company that has all of your needed supplies and information)*

Fungi Fun Facts:

> https://www.bbcearth.com/news/8-fantastic-facts-about-fungi

Mystery mushroom meal

CHAPTER 9

IT'S ALL ABOUT THE COMPOST

GARDEN NOTES

The benefits derived from composting are many. Efficient composting leads to a considerable reduction of the weight in the rubbish bins put out weekly. I have quantified the makeup of a typical trash bin. Between 50 and 75 percent of the contents (by weight) are often able to be composted. Consider that food waste is heavier by comparison than many of the other things that end up in the trash. The material generated by composting (rich, earthy soil) will serve not only as a nutrient boost in your garden but also to improve the overall health of your soil—adding moisture-holding capacity, providing nourishment for invertebrates and microbes, and setting the stage for a more balanced backyard ecosystem. Having a natural fertilizer on hand reduces the need to purchase and apply synthetic fertilizers. The powders and pellets that make up store-bought, manufactured fertilizers are much more likely to run off from your property and end up in the storm drain, which flows out to our waterways and contributes to pollution. You will also save money and time by not having to visit the garden center or hire a contractor for the fertilization of your beds and lawn.

DID YOU KNOW ?

Using compost in your garden not only will provide nutrients but also will hold more water and support soil organisms that are important to the soil and your garden.

Compost pile

To Compost, or Not to Compost	
Compost Yes!	Compost No!
Fruit and Vegetable Scraps	Meat
Eggshells	Dairy
Coffee Grinds	Oils
Unbleached Napkins	Laminated Paper
Chicken, Horse, and Guinea Pig Poo	Dog and Cat Waste
Leaf Litter	Plastics

One of the most common concerns I hear from those who consider composting is "Won't it smell bad?" If you follow a couple of simple rules, this will not be an issue, and your compost bin will smell like the rich, earthy soil that it is destined to become. Add combinations of dry and wet materials. Leaf litter, cardboard (check for any chemical treatments that may have been applied—avoid using if so), and straw can serve as the dry carbon materials, while wet materials are produced largely from your daily food prep. Veggie and fruit scraps, eggshells, and coffee grounds all can be added to the mix. If you are lucky enough to have backyard chickens, the pine shavings and chicken poo make a wonderful addition to your compost heap as well. The list of things not to add is simple: no cat or dog waste, no meat products, and minimize oily materials such as butter and vegetable oil.

Mix your compost regularly. You may choose to have two or three adjacent bins as part of your compost station so that you can move the compost from one stage to the next easily. Make this part of your weekly garden chores—it takes only ten minutes to do. Come spring (and, if you become a composting pro, in the fall as well), you will have lovely, healthy, dark, nutrient-laden soil that will make you and your garden happy—and you will be helping the planet as well!

Compost bins

GARDEN ADVENTURE

It was a spring evening and we had just finished dinner. We were excited about the warmer air that would bring more garden opportunities. Our conversations moved from spring plantings to tools needed to soil preparations. Speaking of soil, I remembered that I needed to take the food waste from the last couple of days out to our compost bins. The sun had set, and I made my way across the garden to the back corner of our yard. I opened the gate, stepped forward, and tossed the contents of our stainless-steel bucket onto the heap on the side of our station that held the raw compost. As the scraps landed, I heard an angry hiss from a creature that had been browsing the contents of the compost. With grizzled gray hair bristling from the interruption of her nighttime forage, she quickly returned to inspecting the offerings, ignoring my presence only a few feet away. I had seen this visitor—an opossum—in our back garden on a number of occasions (I chased her out of our chicken coop only a couple of weeks prior), and I felt bad to have dumped the delivery of compost onto her back. After a short and quiet observation, I returned to the house.

Opossum

Opossums are but one of the creatures drawn to the compost heap. Friends in Maine delight at the occasional visit by a local porcupine. An organic farm I toured in Costa Rica had regular visits from coatis (cousins to the raccoon), who would dine from time to time on the compost. Most mammals that come around are nighttime visitors. If you are a compost enthusiast who would prefer not to see the animals that come to inspect the options, you should deposit your food scraps and garden materials during the day. If you follow the rules of what should and should not go into your compost (see the "Garden Notes" section above), you will reduce the visits of neighborhood animals.

Composting requires a hands-on approach. Regular turnover will help ensure that oxygen is available to the invertebrates and microbes that are working hard to convert your food and garden scraps into valuable natural fertilizer. In my garden the chickens are often one step ahead regarding this chore.

Around the time that the last few tomatoes are harvested for a fall salad and as I gamble on the first frost, waiting for the eggplants to get just a bit bigger before being transformed into a delicious fried-egg-plant sandwich, I am applying the summer compost to the beds. If the compost is layered on top, natural processes—earthworms, rain, and decomposition—will mix the organic material throughout the bed.

Chickens in the compost

When nutrients have been removed from the plot by harvesting fruits and vegetables, the compost will help restore these vital elements.

Around March, as the family is actively planning the upcoming planting, I once again head to the compost heap, always looking to bring someone new outside for the compost tour. I insert a thermometer into the pile. The chill in the air and at the surface of the compost seems to suggest limited activity beneath. But as the thermometer's dial reveals a temperature that the air will not see for another several weeks, evidence of the seemingly magical transformation below is provided. This never ceases to amaze me. and whoever has accompanied me to the garden often contemplates more seriously the many benefits of backyard composting.

I open the gate, wheel in my garden cart, and load the compost from the pile. The spring season has begun, and my seedlings, many of which are still under the grow lights indoors, will be so much better off for the natural fertilizer that awaits in the garden bed. It's all about the compost.

Thermometer inserted in the compost pile

Compost bucket

Beds filled with finished compost

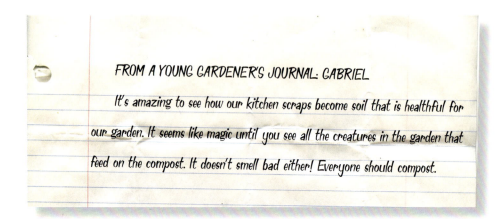

FROM A YOUNG GARDENER'S JOURNAL: GABRIEL

It's amazing to see how our kitchen scraps become soil that is healthful for our garden. It seems like magic until you see all the creatures in the garden that feed on the compost. It doesn't smell bad either! Everyone should compost.

GARDEN ACTIVITY

COMPOST SAFARI

Bring together the kids from the neighborhood, local school, or garden club. Distribute some small containers of fresh compost and some large paintbrushes and spoons. A great way to teach kids about soil, invertebrates, and composting is to have them identify the creatures that find their home in the compost pile.

Golden Guides are a great resource for looking up the creatures they may find. If you have the time, make a creature guide to the compost in advance and have them circle the species they find—a sort of compost scavenger hunt (scavenging for scavengers!).

COMPOST RESOURCES

United States Department of Agriculture's Composting Page:
https://www.usda.gov/peoples-garden/food-access-food-waste/composting

Cornell University Waste Management Institute:
https://cwmi.css.cornell.edu/composting.htm

Natural Resource Defense Council's Composting Page:
https://www.nrdc.org/stories/composting-101#whatis

Planet Natural Research Center—Compost Creatures:
https://www.planetnatural.com/composting-101/science/biology/

CHAPTER 10

GARDEN FOR NATURE

GARDEN NOTES

Gardens would not exist without nature. The cycling of nutrients, the availability of water, the pollination of flowers, and the building of soil all require processes and organisms to ensure that the basic needs of a garden plot are met. If we hope to improve the harvest and maintain the healthiest garden possible, we must pay attention to what nature teaches us and practice the methods of gardening that support both our food plants and the living things that make gardens possible.

Take a moment to watch your garden. Do not simply admire the pending harvest or the organization of your plants in the plot; closely examine the inhabitants of the edible habitat. Remember that your garden not only benefits you but also provides many resources to the diversity of life found there. You will see an amazing variety of creatures! Some will be obvious. I delight at seeing our resident groundhog amble into the garden, browsing the possible dining options while also keeping a lookout for our dog, who keeps these feeding visits short (and keeps me from being overly nervous about losing all of our crops). Though our backyard chickens are often preoccupied with exploring the wilder parts of our backyard, they do, on occasion, come around to inspect the vegetable beds, which are surrounded by a raised border that keeps all but the very edges almost out of reach of our flock. The chickens do find a tasty morsel from time to time and are happy to peck an unsuspecting insect from the leaves of our tomato plants. The robins and grackles will work the soil in the garden as well, scratching around for a meal. For the most part, the resident wildlife does not alter our garden activities, though one spring we had to abandon a raised garden when a rabbit decided to nest under the cantaloupe leaves. Smart bunny—food and shelter all in the same space!

Butterfly on a flower

Groundhog

Isopod

But most of the species in our garden beds are not mammals and birds. As in all ecosystems, invertebrates dominate the community. Easily dismissed as "bugs," invertebrates include a wide variety of creatures. Worms, centipedes and millipedes, spiders, crustaceans, and mollusks, along with insects, make up the bulk of garden biodiversity. You are likely more familiar with some of these creatures in other habitats and perhaps did not know that they live in your garden! Crustaceans and mollusks are common in marine and freshwater habitats. Millipedes and centipedes are found in forests, while spiders occupy meadows. The garden habitat provides the same types of resources that these species require in what we might describe as more natural habitats. Their presence in our garden beds, however, tells us that our backyards can be just as beneficial a habitat as the wilder places we might travel to visit.

Millipede

Not only can we support the presence of these visitors or residents of our garden, but we should! When we support nature, nature supports us! This can be done in our garden beds. Using natural fertilizers (compost and manure) and avoiding the use of pesticides will provide healthful food and healthy habitat. Diversifying the variety of plants in our garden will also make flowers available for pollinators at different times during the growing season. These simple actions will keep insect populations healthy and, in turn, will help balance the entire backyard habitat, even beyond your garden plots.

If you want to focus even more on supporting wildlife in your garden, you can plan other spaces for them as well. Perhaps the easiest way to do this is to set aside areas of your property where nature is simply allowed to grow wild. How much of the garden space you can designate as "wild" depends on how close you are to your neighbors and the other features of your garden. If you live very close to other properties, discuss with your neighbors your goals for wildlife. Maybe they will join in, and you can create a community effort for establishing wild gardens! If neighbors are not so keen on wilder spaces, maybe reduce the size of your natural plots or tuck those areas out of sight from others. Chances are, no matter how big or small, you can have a patch of wilderness in your garden!

Wild garden

Want to get involved in active restoration for wildlife? Then a pollinator wildlife garden may be for you. These are gardens designed with specific plants that are beneficial for species that require flowers for their food, nectar, and pollen. Some are designed with a specific species in mind, such as milkweed plants for monarch butterflies. Others are designed as general pollinator gardens with the goal of supporting a wide variety of species. Insects and other invertebrates may require food from other plant parts and of course may take up residence in a garden as well. As such, plantings and other features such as stones, sticks, flowerpots, water sources, mulch, and various other habitats could add to the quality of the wildlife-friendly space. If you are planning to support birds and other vertebrates, consider small trees, fruiting shrubs, rock features, and housing that may encourage birds, bats, reptiles, and other animals to occupy the garden. Each of these species will contribute to the balance of your garden ecosystem.

Garter snake

Consider that your garden, by location or specific feature, may also have benefits beyond providing for biodiversity. A rain garden planted in a low spot on your property can capture rainfall and reduce the runoff of water into storm sewers while increasing groundwater recharge (water moving down through the soils that can be used by plants or people). Gardens along the sidewalk or street can keep soil in place, preventing the loss of soil by erosion. In the end, planting gardens for nature not only will provide habitat for wildlife but will also improve the aesthetic appeal of your property and make for a healthier environment.

DID YOU KNOW ?

A healthy garden provides benefits to nature and people. Pollination, nutrient cycling, soil health, preventing erosion—all of these are what are known as ecosystem services. We cannot live without these processes provided by other species!

Bee landing on milkweed

It hardly seemed like the best weather day for gardening. Clouds were pushed along by a strong wind, keeping the time between sun and shade brief. It was March, and though the past couple of days had been warmer than usual, the calendar still said winter. In our hearts and minds we were still in garden mode. It wasn't often that we could get the whole group together. About ten kids huddled together for warmth as we outlined the goals for the day. This was the second year for this pollinator garden in our town. Along a straight stretch of public green space where a train used to run to Philadelphia, there were various features and activity stations for residents and visitors. Many years ago, a large section of the mile-long path was bordered by a meadow, but it had been long since removed for reasons uncertain. Our Junior Naturalist Club has set out to restore these habitats for the benefit of people, plants, and wildlife. Building off successes and lessons learned in our own gardens, with the advice of Ernst Conservation Seed, and inspired by the conservation work of the Xerces Society and National Wildlife Federation, we have established four pollinator/wildlife gardens along the path in our town. These gardens have been the focus of artistic and scientific study in our community. Additionally, it is quite often that I see people sitting adjacent to the gardens and sharing a picnic, resting, or simply observing the aesthetic value of the gardens.

Merchantville Gardens

With a vibrant art community in our town, photographers, painters, and other artists have used the gardens and their inhabitants as the subjects of study. These works have been shared within families and neighborhoods and used for educational programs and in promotional presentations to advocate for more restoration and planting.

The Junior Naturalist Club members have been involved in every step of the pollinator garden project. The members participated in site selection, which involved soil inspection

Garden-inspired art by Gabe

and ground measurements to ensure we planted in areas with enough buffer space for recreation and other uses of the greenway. They helped select the seed mix we would plant, considering the benefits for different groups of animals and the sun and soil conditions of the site. The team prepared the site, removing invasive plants and adding compost soil to the ground, and the club members planted the seeds and installed a temporary rope boundary to keep the site from being disturbed.

Our garden lessons emphasized the need to monitor the gardens. We have assessed which plant species have succeeded, which invasive plants have returned, and the diversity of invertebrates and other species that have benefited from the plantings. We set up simple experiments and studies to answer questions that the kids have asked. Curious

The Junior Naturalist Club's pollinator garden

about how many milkweed plants would grow after planting two thousand seeds in one of the gardens during the fall, the naturalist club members counted the milkweed plants present in the garden the following summer. They determined that about 3 percent of the planted seeds grew into mature plants that could provide food and habitat for invertebrates in the garden. Additionally, in true naturalist style, the group has identified curious relationships that form between insects and the plants in the garden. Many of the goldenrod plants in the garden have roundish swellings on their stems. By using nets and iNaturalist, we solved the mystery of what we were observing: goldenrod galls!

Goldenrod with gall

DID YOU KNOW ?

Some plants, such as goldenrod, will house larval insects that live within their stems or leaves. The plant will form the gall—often round and fibrous—in response to the presence of the insect. The typical goldenrod galls on the stem (easily visible in winter) are created by the goldenrod gall fly.

The seasonal changes in the garden have revealed the variety of species that are active in these restored habitats. Bumblebees emerge and are often among the first to arrive in the spring, taking advantage of the first blooms to bring color to the garden. On warm summer evenings, the garden is host to the concert of crickets. Migrating monarch butterflies touch down in fall as they travel from all over the Northeast to destinations farther south. Though insect activity is quiet in the winter, juncos and white-throated sparrows can be seen kicking up seeds among the leaf piles that are caught in the dried stems of the meadow plants.

Lessons in conservation are practiced in these pollinator gardens. Like for any garden, upkeep is required. We carefully remove nonnative species that would tend to take over the plots.

On more than one occasion, a neighbor or passerby along the bike path adjacent to these gardens has asked why we leave the gardens looking so "messy" in the fall and through the winter. Why are all the leaves not raked and removed and the dead plants not cut down? The answer is ecological! Leaves and dead plants offer

Dark-eyed junco

food and habitat to winter visitors to the garden and are essentially a blanket for the soil, where many invertebrates are overwintering. In addition, the leaf litter and plant roots keep the soil in place, are a source of spring nutrients, and will help retain water needed by plants and animals alike.

I love a bit of honey in my tea. This sweet, delicious, thick, golden liquid—what some may consider merely a sugary treat—belies an interesting reality. Nature's sugar has many benefits for human health. Researchers continue to explore the potential of honey in boosting the immune system, helping to contribute to heart health, and promoting various other potential benefits when included in a healthful diet. Produced by bees, honey is the energy source these insects use to maintain the hive, fly,

Mugwort in the pollinator garden

and build the colony. Since ancient times, for over five thousand years, people have kept hives to pollinate crops and harvest honey.

On an early-fall day, we were invited out to one of the farms serviced by Mill Creek Apiary, a local family-owned company that provides pollinator services and offers a variety of bee-based products, from honey to wax to skin care products. Jason, the owner of Mill Creek, arranged for us to visit on a day when he was checking the hives. As we

DID YOU KNOW ?

The place where hives are kept to raise bees is known as an apiary, and beekeepers are known as apiarists.

Hives of Mill Creek Apiary

Honeybee

walked along a wooden fence that separated farm cows from a field adjacent to a forest patch, the rows of white boxes appeared lifeless. We noticed bees working a patch of goldenrod and asters. As bees lifted their pollen loads from flowers, they seemed to guide us toward Jason, who stood near the dozen or so wooden hives. They were—to use a bee reference—buzzing with activity!

After a brief introduction to the life cycle of bees, the structure of the hives, the benefits of honey, and the tools that Jason and his team use to maintain the hives, we were invited to suit up. A bee suit protects the beekeeper from being stung; its bee shirt and gloves, along with a hooded veil that covers the head and face, are designed to keep the bees from exposed skin. Jason introduced the smoker, which is a small metal can that puffs out wispy clouds of smoke that calm the bees. Removing the top cover of the hive and lifting a frame—alive with bees—from the inside, Jason revealed the busy workers. We all stood in a circle around Jason, nearly close enough to touch the hive, as he revealed hundreds of bees covering the comb that embedded the frame. Jason brushed a few bees aside to show us the comb with

Jason from Mill Creek Apiary

honey, where the bees were amazingly docile. One even landed on my hand (I was not wearing gloves), crawled about for a few seconds, and then went back to work.

Jason made it look easy. He had revealed the details of a day in the life of an apiarist, and we all gained a great respect both for the bees and the beekeeper. To protect the honeybees, and all insects, for that matter, it is essential to consider the surrounding landscape. Proper hive maintenance, avoiding pesticide use, and protecting both bees and habitat all are essential preparations and ongoing requirements for the beekeeper. Keeping bees is not for the casual backyard gardener but for those interested in the art and science of bees, pollination, and hives. With the required training, education, and dedication, beekeeping may be a wonderful addition to your garden.

Learn more about bee and invertebrate conservation at www.xerces.org.

Gabe with smoker

DID YOU KNOW ?

There are over 20,000 bee species worldwide, and we must be sure to protect the habitat of wild species. There must be a balance between keeping bees to enhance local farm and garden pollination while ensuring the conservation of wild species as well!

Goldenrod, a late-summer bloom

FROM A YOUNG GARDENER'S JOURNAL: THE DUNN FAMILY

Our trip to the apiary was so much fun. We put on bee suits, used a smoker to calm the bees, and got to look inside the hive. We actually spotted the queen! The honey we sampled came from a local cranberry farm.

Suited up: outfitted in a bee suit

GARDEN ACTIVITY

PLANNING YOUR POLLINATOR GARDEN

The following pollinators are regular visitors to backyard gardens. Look up the plants that these insects require as a food source or host plant for their eggs and larvae. List three plants for each insect and identify the species that are needed by the most insects.

Insect Pollinators:

> monarch butterfly
> bumblebee
> soldier beetle
> hawk moth
> hoverfly
> potter wasp

GARDEN RESOURCES

Xerces Society:

> https://www.xerces.org

National Wildlife Federation Backyard Habitat:

> https://www.nwf.org/CERTIFY

Ernst Conservation Seeds:

> https://www.ernstseed.com/

DID YOU KNOW ?

Bees have been the inspiration of books, movies, and artwork. One of my favorite creative productions is this video, "For the Bees": https://www.youtube.com/watch?v=r99iCk1boFs.

— CHAPTER 11 —

COMMUNITY GARDEN

GARDEN ACTIVITY

I recently took a trip to the Chesapeake Bay. Heading south from the Philadelphia area, we were happy to leave behind the interstate and take the back roads. Taking the back roads is something my family always did; though it added some time on to our trip, it would always offer something interesting to see and, quite simply, a more pleasant ride to our destination. As an educator, community scientist, and someone who celebrates an adventure, I love to describe landscapes and unique features of the places I visit and compare the experiences from different explorations.

On this late-spring day, the weather was clear following overnight rain. A breeze was blowing, and the landscape responded. For what seemed like miles, alternating fields of young corn and soy swayed in the wind, and under the ideal growing conditions of moist soil and bright sunshine, you could almost see the plants rising toward the sun.

DID YOU KNOW ?
Corn is a type of grass!

Monocrop of corn

Agricultural landscapes appear to be a celebration of the earth's bounty. Green fields and rich soil can support a harvest that feeds the people of our towns, cities, and planet. But on this day, what we observed brought an interesting fact to our day's travel adventure. No people! We did not see a single person working the fields, driving a tractor, or staffing a roadside stand. In addition, the transition from one field to another did not include any natural habitats. We saw distant stands of trees and crossed small bridges under which water flowed, but most plots were separated only by barren sandy paths, irrigation pipes, or paved roads.

Farm Practice (by acreage) in the United States

Organic
1.0%

Conventional (non-organic)
99.0%

Rancocas Creek Farm

The very nature of a farm connects to community. It takes an ecological community of species to support the farm: insects to pollinate, trees to support the predators of farm pests, worms to aerate the ground, and microbes to cycle the nutrients. The planting, harvest, and delivery of food require the efforts of people, but perhaps too often our modern agricultural practices operate in ways that reduce the need for community.

As I recall the years I spent with my grandfather in his garden, with constant discussion and interaction with the soil, water, plants, organisms, and visiting friends and neighbors, I can't help but compare those memories with our observations of these monocrop fields devoid of people and wildlife and feel sorry for these farms. Beyond emphasizing the importance of supporting natural processes and biodiversity to sustain healthy gardens, farms, and the planet, we should also embrace the idea that growing food and working together on farm projects can bring people together and improve communication, collaboration, and physical and emotional well-being—and, I would establish, create a more peaceful coexistence for humanity. Perhaps one might say this is an exaggeration of the potential benefits of expanding and developing the farm and garden community, but I firmly believe in its power.

During those many summers working my grandfather's garden plots, I would meet many of his neighbors and friends, who would always leave with an armful of produce and a smile on their face from having shared stories, conversation, and helpful hints on gardening. In addition, local fishermen would bring my grandfather the bones and other leftovers from their catch after they harvested the filets. This material would be added to the soil to enhance the yield for next season's crops. Strangers walking by would quickly become connected to the garden community as their questions and compliments would lead to stories and conversations. It is clear to me now that my grandfather's garden was the roots of an ever-expanding community in the town where he lived.

As an educator, I have come to embrace gardens for building community within and beyond our schools. Our annual seed sale and crop-seedling program has connected students with their families in establishing gardens. Our environmental program has connected with the town by offering educational opportunities on composting and organic practices, and our science classes have connected with the other academic departments at the school through writing, art projects, and mathematical approaches to our experimental soil and crop studies. Our community pollinator gardens have enhanced the aesthetics of the school campus and public spaces, and sustainability efforts have been celebrated by our Sustainable Jersey partner groups in town.

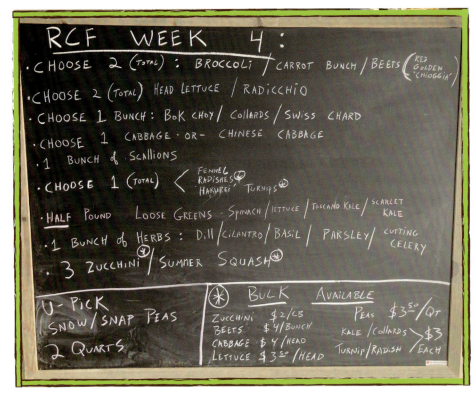

Offerings at the CSA

Community pollinator garden

Sign for Merchantville Community Garden

Cheeses produced from the Saul School in Philadelphia

Urban gardens at Norris Square Neighborhood Project

The school district of Philadelphia has an agricultural campus, the Walter B. Saul High School, which offers full programs in agriculture ranging from horticulture to animal science to natural resource management. Their classes, events, and programs bring farming and related activities into the community of Philadelphia and work to develop the connections between our urban environments and farming. Elsewhere in Philadelphia, the Farm Philly Program supports dozens of agricultural projects throughout the city.

These programs engage children, help set up community gardens, establish compositing initiatives, offer space for growing plants from seeds in a community greenhouse, and promote sustainable connections to the natural world. As of 2022, the city has drafted its first-ever Urban Agriculture Strategic Plan. Closer to my home, the City of Camden, New Jersey, has also invested in urban gardens with the Center for Environmental Transformation. Along with Rutgers University, this program establishes and promotes urban agriculture, training, and projects across the city.

It is not just in big cities where gardens and farming can transform the community. In my town of Merchantville, we have a small but growing community garden. About a dozen families have plots in our local park, where a variety of crops are grown and shared. Our Organic Gardens program is enhanced by another initiative, Edible Merchantville, which works to bring locally produced food into the community-shared spaces and donates surplus produce to local charities. It is just these types of initiatives that put the community in community gardens!

Ezra from Rancocas Creek Farm

Within an hour's drive in any direction, despite living in an urban location, we can access a variety of farms. A growing number of these farms encourage visitors and offer pick-your-own produce and programs to teach anyone about sustainability and food. These are the programs in the cities and rural areas close to my home. Check out and get involved in the events and programs that are near where you live!

GARDEN ADVENTURE

FARM VISIT

We entered the gate of Rancocas Creek Farm on a cool, early October morning. Our members of the Junior Naturalist Club were excited about the visit to this sustainable farm adjacent to the headquarters of Pinelands Preservation Alliance in Southampton, New Jersey. In 2020, this farm, which had previously been a soybean farm growing only a single crop using conventional methods (pesticides and chemical fertilizers), was donated to Pinelands Preservation Alliance. It has been rapidly transformed into a productive and sustainable farm ecosystem that emphasizes natural growing methods and diversity both in its crops and its landscape.

The day's visit would focus on every element of the farm community, from preparing the fields, to the diversity of crops, to the management of pests, to the involvement of the community. After a brief history of the site and introductions to the farm staff, including interns and volunteers, we walked past a vintage tractor, which seemed to symbolize the return to simpler times and practices in farming, on our way to the first stop on our tour.

Old farm tractor

DID YOU KNOW ?

Farms such as Rancocas Creek Farm have CSAs (community-supported agriculture), which allows people to buy shares of produce from the farm and, in some cases, volunteer hours on the farm in exchange for produce.

We walked up to a garden of wildflowers. A beautiful assortment of fall blooms, they are offered as a pick-your-own option to CSA members of the farm and provided the opportunity to be part of the farm harvest. Ecologically, the flowers provided forage and habitat to a diversity of insects, whose presence on the farm provided essential pollination services to the rotation of crops that would be planted from early spring through the fall. This first farm lesson captures well the key concepts learned on this visit: sustainable farms are about more than just the food crops.

As we followed the bees, butterflies, and beetles moving from one flower to another in the colorful field, we were moving toward rows of plants that, from a distance, also provided an intense splash of color. Peppers hung from the leafy branches of plants that stood about waist high. The abundance of fruit was impressive, with each plant supporting dozens of shiny red peppers. Closer inspection revealed that the peppers were of different sizes and shapes. Ezra, one of the farm interns, explained that by growing various types of peppers, the farm staff could endure limited harvest from one type if insects or other challenges reduced the success of the crop. A benefit of biodiversity!

Diverse crops at RCF

RCF blooms

Red peppers

The next plot to visit was across a low, wet depression, which was planted with young trees and other types of plants. This site, though not growing crops, was still planted with purpose. Prior to the start of Rancocas Creek Farm, the field would regularly experience erosion, because rainwater runoff would leave the property along a low depression that flows toward a local stream. With little vegetation to hold the soil in place, tons of soil were being lost every season. This reduced the fertility of the land, since topsoil holds nutrients. Plus, the washed-away sediment would ultimately end up in the stream, polluting the aquatic ecosystem. The diversity of the trees, shrubs, and other plants that now cover this low spot on the farm hold the soil in place, reducing the energy of flowing water, capturing more water that can then enter the ground, and offering habitat to wildlife on the farm property.

We passed by the blackberry patch, now devoid of the tasty fresh fruit that was a favorite of farmers and patrons alike (not to mention the local birds). One of the junior naturalists asked about how animals that would want to eat the crops were kept away. Chris, the other intern, pointed behind the group. Tall poles supported the white, tiered houses that offered an apartment-style living for birds. These were purple martin nesting boxes. These agile birds are social nesters; in the eastern United States, they almost exclusively nest in hollow gourds, nesting boxes, and other structures established by people to attract the insectivorous birds to a given site. Their presence provides natural insect control and helps keep in check the populations of invertebrates that enjoy snacking on

Blackberry time!

Sharp-shinned hawk

the variety of plants growing at any time on the farm. As for the birds and other animals that might like to partake in some fruits and vegetables, certainly some produce may be lost to their foraging habits. However, the farm design resembles an ecosystem. There is diversity of habitat, and the variety of crops does not allow any single pest population to increase to levels that would destroy an entire harvest. Diversity of crops leads to a diversity of species that might take advantage of available food. At the same time, diversity of habitats also brings a diversity of predators—snakes, hawks, foxes, and various invertebrates—that will help manage the species that dine on farm plants.

Moving on, our next stop was a field of plants that no one in our group recognized. Small white flowers were abundant atop the heart-shaped leaves. Upon close inspection, we observed a few bees drop down onto the flowers. We now had a hint as to its purpose. Buckwheat is a fast-growing grain-like crop that is used both as a food source and a cover crop. I have had buckwheat pancakes before, but I had never seen the plant that produces the kernels (called groats) that are mixed in with flour for this breakfast food.

Cover crop plot (on right) next to pepper plants

Growing well in cool weather, the seeds will grow quickly into mature plants with flowers. Not only does this plant protect the soil and offer flowers to pollinators, but it also will help keep insects from accessing other plants nearby (its thick growth can be a challenge for insects to negotiate). This amazing crop can also be food for humans and livestock. So, if it grows a bit too quickly or simply grows in abundance, harvest some for your backyard flock (yes, another endorsement for backyard chickens). Additionally, this crop can be cut at the end of the season and worked into the soil, since the nutrients from its decay will then be available to next year's crops.

Clover

Cover crops were not the only natural fertilizer source at the farm. As we strolled along, there seemed to be compost everywhere. Crop leftovers from the farm were mulched in with wood chips and various other plant materials made for heaps of organic fertilizer, which can be applied to the plots to support plant growth and enrich the soil.

DID YOU KNOW ?

Cover crops are used to reduce erosion, restore nutrients in the soil, and provide food for pollinators and other species.

DID YOU KNOW ?

A group of pigs are called a drift or drove.

Our final stop on the tour was a crowd favorite. A drift of pigs enthusiastically awaited our arrival as we walked down the fence line toward the pen. The ground was a broken mosaic of exposed muddy soil and turned-over weeds. Pigs are good excavators and make their mark quickly in the area where they are kept. A few wallows were filled with saturated mud, and some of the pigs wore the soil stains of their enjoyment after rolling about in these depressions.

Our tour guides handed out to the kids apples that were not fit for sale. The kids delighted in tossing the fruit to the waiting pigs. Both pigs and kids celebrated the interaction as our group tried to make sure that the treats were distributed evenly among the eager swine. Somehow the same few pigs seemed to anticipate where the next tossed apple would land. The oinks and grunts of those that came up short were entertaining. After ensuring that every pig received at least one apple, the junior naturalists asked many questions about pig care, growth, and the eventual fate of the pigs. The hope from our junior naturalist was that the pigs were pets and efficient consumers of leftovers on the farm. The mood turned solemn when the honest answer revealed that these pigs would be food in the coming months. This was an important

RCF pigs

reality to the kids. Some of our group had never been to a farm and had never met animals that would be food. As we walked away from the pen, one student pledged that she would not eat bacon ever again. Whether or not this promise would be kept, the visit to Rancocas Creek Farm was an important lesson in the ecology of our food.

After a picnic lunch at the farm, we left for home. Lessons learned would be applied to the backyards and community gardens back in our town. Inspired by pollination, compost, cover crops, and pigs, we were wiser stewards of our garden plots—however big or small.

FROM A YOUNG GARDENER'S JOURNAL: GABRIEL

I have visited Rancocas Creek Farm during every season. There were so many different crops at the farm. It was interesting to see what they are growing. The garlic was underground, and then, once they harvested it, it was hung from the ceiling in the shed!

Gabe with pigs

Garlic in the rafters

GARDEN ACTIVITY

YOUR COMMUNITY FARMS

Complete a web search of your local or regional farms. Depending on where you live, consider surrounding towns or perhaps a countywide search. List their products and activities (what they grow and any special programs they have, such as CSA or pick-your-own opportunities).

Access Google Earth and measure the distance of each farm to your immediate community, school, or neighborhood.

Google Earth has a project feature that allows you to develop a slide sequence of stops along a Google Earth tour. Find the tutorial here: https://www.google.com/earth/outreach/learn/create-a-map-or-story-in-google-earth-web/.

Other educational resources are available here: https://www.google.com/earth/education/resources/.

Create a Google Earth project tour of farms in your region for your family or class or nature center. Organize a tour of a farm or two to educate friends, family members, and classmates on the community connections to food and farming.

Community Agriculture:
https://www.nal.usda.gov/farms-and-agricultural-production-systems/community-supported-agriculture

Find a Community Supported Agriculture Option:
https://www.localharvest.org/

Community garden in full bloom

PART THREE

GARDEN LESSONS

CHAPTER 12

THE CLASSROOM GARDEN

GARDEN NOTES

As a young person, I never connected school with my adventures outside. Though I knew I was taught a great deal from my grandfather in his garden, the mushroom lady in the woods near my home, and the farm manager who showed me the most efficient way to pick blueberries on the farm where I worked as a teenager, this was not school. I considered my time learning about wild food, crops, and garden techniques to be practical, fun, interesting, and adventurous. Quite simply, I would not have described most activities in school to be any of these things. To be clear, I liked my teachers and enjoyed going to school. Recess with my friends, the occasional spelling bee, holiday concerts—all these were enjoyable, but I saw the day-to-day learning merely as what you did as a kid. I guess I looked at my presence in the classroom as kind of a contractual arrangement. The teachers teach and the students learn.

The only time that food was a part of school was lunchtime with my friends and the occasional bake sale to support some school project or trip. Thinking back, we always watched the clock when it was approaching lunch, and had to coordinate signups when it came to bake sales. Fresh fruits and vegetables were seldom part of my school activities or on the menu at lunch. In my family, the scramble to get five children out the door to school limited the lunch-packing process in the morning. There was active trading that would occur around the lunch table, but fresh carrot sticks did not hold much value. Bake sales required a scramble on the weekend to use a box of premixed ingredients for brownies or cookies, to prepare a sweet treat that could fetch a quarter on the foldout table in the school hallway. Participation in bake sales may have included the occasional recipe that called for raisins, but my preparations were always challenging, even when

Brown-bag lunch

the ingredients came from a box, let alone adding some dried fruit to the mix.

In contemplating the lessons offered by my grandfather and other adults from whom I learned about growing and harvesting food, I now realize just how many subjects were truly at the core of a garden experience. Rooting through the compost pile in search of bugs was an informal lesson in taxonomy and feeding roles in nature: there were predators, detritivores, herbivores, and omnivores scavenging about the assortment of food scraps. Working the compost into the soil and filling in low-lying areas that would collect too much water involved earth science concepts: soil particle size, infiltration, and percolation of water. Adding broken seashells to the soil adjusted the chemistry, making growing conditions more favorable for the crops. As it turns out, the soil on this barrier island was naturally very acidic. Spring and fall crops would be grown in areas of the garden where the available sun would still provide enough light for photosynthesis. Examining the hardiness zones would inform us on when certain seeds or seedlings could be planted. These activities required knowledge of geography, day length, and sunlight angle changes per season.

A compost bin we built

The stories of crops and seeds brought to this country from the gardens of my great-grandparents revealed the stories of my family—their culture, their food, and their daily activities. Reading about the origins of the New Jersey blueberry industry in the early 1900s gave me perspective on human history and the early role of women in science. Even my meager sales of berries from the card table stand at the end of the driveway brought lessons in finance.

From the meals we would share, to the menus we would plan, to the neighbors we would share our harvest with, every aspect of our garden adventures had numerous academic and life lessons.

DID YOU KNOW ?

Earth is tilted on its axis, and this is what brings us our seasons!

DID YOU KNOW ?

The hardiness zones have recently been redrawn as the climate has changed in the last couple of decades.

Seeds germinating

Handwritten seed packs

GARDEN ADVENTURE

As part of my work in science education and the environmental projects for which I volunteer, I have come to realize the value of food—diversity, planting, harvesting, sharing, and enjoying—both in the academic as well as the social and wellness aspects of teaching. For the better part of three months at the beginning of the school year, I lead my students through various topics and investigations in ecology. Perhaps there is no easier way for us to examine the connections of our lives to the natural world than through the food that we purchase, prepare, and consume. The ecology of a farm or backyard garden must be examined if we are to be successful gardeners.

With focus on the importance of pollinators, you can prepare an assortment of food items that are possible thanks only to the services of bees, beetles, butterflies, wasps, and flies. Consider preparing a plate of pollinator-provided food that children are likely to find familiar: carrots, apples, berries, melons, cucumbers, peppers, garlic, and even chocolate! In the United States alone, over a hundred crops are pollinated by insects. Students can take inventory of all the fruits and vegetables that require pollination—either for the edible parts of the plant or for the production of the seeds that will bring about next year's crop.

The origins of food crops bring into focus geography, climate, and human history. While enjoying a homemade pizza (the toppings were supplied from our garden), we discussed the origins of pizza. A bit of research led us to the fact that flatbreads (the precursor to the official pizza pie) were very popular in ancient times, enjoyed by the Egyptians, Romans, and Greeks. The origins of the pizza that many of us recognize—with tomato sauce and cheese—came from the west coast of Italy. But what about the tomatoes used in the sauce? Turns out, tomatoes can be traced back to South America!

One of the favorite treats I would make with my grandfather was apple pie. To this day, I establish that no one makes a better pie than he did (I like to think I come close to matching his recipe). We loved picking the apples that would be used in our baking. Apples are not native to the forests of the mid-Atlantic and New England—places where I have spent time in backyard orchards harvesting fruit. Instead, they are from Asia, having been transported to Europe around five hundred or so years ago and then on to North America in the centuries that would follow.

DID YOU KNOW ?

Mosquito species are effective pollinators of the tiny flowers of the cacao tree, the plant that produces chocolate!

Common fresh fruits and veggies that require pollinators

Schools can establish gardens as part of community partnerships or academic initiatives. A local elementary school is granted a plot in our town community garden. Not only does this provide the kids with opportunities to prepare their plots, sow seeds, observe the growth of their crops, and then harvest, but they also have the opportunity to interact with other community gardeners, observing the diversity of the plots, learning about irrigation and pollination, and participating in the production of local compost.

If a garden plot is not available due to space or partnership, indoor growing is another possibility. There are hydroponic kits that can be purchased or built to use indoors; with enough sun, planter gardens are possible as well. The preparation of soil, the selection and planting of seeds, and the varied growing conditions for the crops can be studied. During the last weeks of winter in my classroom, we make paper pots from old wrapping paper or newspaper and carry out controlled experiments investigating varied soil types and treatments to determine how seed germination and seedling growth respond to the varied conditions. This maximizes the scientific study, while also producing hundreds of garden seedlings for the home gardens of my students. Additionally, we have sold our seedlings as a fundraiser for local conservation organizations and have given away plants during our annual Earth Day Fair.

Mini gala apple

Emphasis on sustainability is a must when it comes to agricultural and garden ecology and production. Think about how many of the food items you purchase and consume could be grown locally. What do they require to produce? Are there ways to increase production while still remaining sustainable (protecting soil and water resources as well as protecting biodiversity)? We can investigate ways to irrigate, ways to remove weedy plants that may crowd out our crops, and ways to provide additional nutrients without using commercial fertilizers. Many of these questions can be examined through scientific study, observation, and data collection. Once again, we identify that the practice of science can be satisfied through interdisciplinary investigations involving gardens!

A greenhouse classroom

Paper-pot seedling soil study

Norris Street Project, an urban garden

Community gardens and local farms can produce a surprising diversity and amount of food. When this food is shared with and distributed to those in need, we help bridge food and nutrition gaps in our neighborhoods and cities and improve environmental justice.

Examining the state of food waste in our schools and communities can shed light on an issue that could be addressed with thoughtful planning and programs that work to identify where excess food is located and where it could be distributed.

The lessons of food in the classroom can enhance skills, improve community, identify food insecurity issues, and empower students to engage the elements of food science, food culture, and the connections between food and people.

Assessment of High School Cafeteria Waste Bins After Lunch

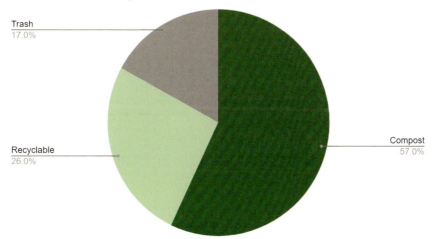

Trash
17.0%

Recyclable
26.0%

Compost
57.0%

Gabe's boots

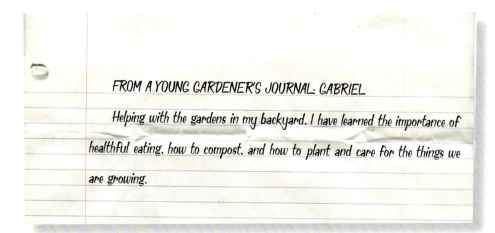

FROM A YOUNG GARDENER'S JOURNAL: GABRIEL

Helping with the gardens in my backyard, I have learned the importance of healthful eating, how to compost, and how to plant and care for the things we are growing.

A diverse harvest

GARDEN ACTIVITY

SUSTAINABLE RESOURCES

Many of the resources we need to use to keep our food production sustainable and healthful for people and nature are renewable resources.

Identify the renewable resources that are essential to a backyard or school/community garden. What problems could occur regarding the availability or quality of these resources? Design a controlled study to address an idea to improve sustainability and reduce the environmental impact from the use of one of these resources.

GARDEN RESOURCES

Growing Minds—Steps to a Classroom Garden:
https://growing-minds.org/steps-to-a-classroom-garden/

Kids Gardening—Connecting the Garden to the Classroom:
https://kidsgardening.org/resources/
create-sustain-a-program-connecting-the-garden-to-the-classroom-2/#

CHAPTER 13

LET'S GET PLANTING!

GARDEN NOTES

Why do you want to start a garden? Perhaps you are interested in growing your own food? Do you want to join with friends to start a community program? Do you want to lower your ecological footprint? Or do you want to study and teach about nature and natural processes? Are you interested in building a school program on sustainable food?

All these things can be accomplished through gardening. Like other activities that may be new to you, it can be daunting to start. Here are a few recommendations to get you moving in the right direction by starting simple and staying the course.

Set realistic goals for your gardening. Like other adventures in life, there will be unexpected challenges, new ideas, and wonderful surprises. The bottom line is that growing your own food or tending to a patch of flowers will bring you closer to nature and will teach you much about the environment, other species, your friends and family, and yourself! No matter how big or small your yard, whether you are maintaining a couple of potted plants or a maze of diverse crops woven into the landscape of your backyard, gardens will bring you joy!

Your garden journey may result in increasing the amount of natural space in your yard as you seek to increase the habitat of beneficial backyard species that will pollinate and control the outbreaks of occasional pests. Your focus will turn to the basic elements and changes that

DID YOU KNOW ?

Via www.footprintcalculator.org, you can measure your ecological footprint to find out how food choices and garden activities can reduce your impact on the earth.

Homemade grow box with herbs

each season brings. You will monitor morning temperatures in early spring, manage periods of heavy rain and periods of drought, and provide the occasional fortification should the wind challenge your plots. Observation is your best tool, but resources are always a good idea. Browse extension websites (see the resources at the end of this chapter) and garden pages of organizations that specialize in growing the types of plants you have in your beds.

Good soil is important to successful gardening.

If you are new to gardening, or if your garden plots have been used for many years, you may need to assess the soil in your plots. There are three basic nutrients that are needed in significant quantities in your soil. Nitrogen, phosphorus, and potassium (often simply abbreviated as NPK) are needed by your plants in order to stay healthy and produce flowers, leaves, and fruits. Various other elements are needed as well. In addition to soil nutrients, the pH of the soil (how acidic or basic) is another important property. Certain crops (such as blueberries) grow well under acidic conditions while other crops require a neutral pH (neither too acidic nor too basic). The texture of the soil can affect how well water can get to roots and how much water the soil can hold. Generally speaking, soil with adequate amounts of organic material—broken down from organisms, from additions of compost, or both—in balance with sand, silt, and some clay results in a soil (called loam) that many plants find agreeable. To determine the soil nutrient content and pH, kits can be obtained from extension offices or garden centers (again, see the resources at the end of this chapter). Regarding soil texture, improvements can be made by adding compost or enriched topsoil material from a local garden center. Talk to local professionals about your goals.

DID YOU KNOW ?

Inspecting a handful of soil can tell you quite a bit about moisture content, texture, and organic content.

A handful of soil

DID YOU KNOW ?

The three main particle sizes for soil minerals are sand, silt, and clay. Sand is the largest of the three, while clay is the smallest. Sand is the most porous and clay the least. A combination of the three is generally good for the garden.

Invest in your tools. I know some gardeners who like to have every gadget that can do something unique (dibblers, seed tampers, bed rulers, pot brushes, and widgets). My grandfather had a hand shovel, shears, a hoe, an old watering can, and a pair of leather work gloves—that's it. These

A dibbler

are the items that are must-haves to perform the daily tasks in the garden. Other tools may be useful, and you may choose to develop your tool kit, but I recommend starting with the basics. Whenever possible, I like to support the local garden shops.

If learning is as important to you as the harvest that comes from your garden, your preparations may focus more on the process. Again, cooperative extensions and local garden clubs are great resources. If you are working with kids, simplicity will likely enhance the experience and greatly improve your chances for success. Access to a greenhouse can extend not only the growing season, but the opportunities for fixing mistakes. Space, budget, and time all are important considerations when planning your garden, but never let limitations keep you from the garden. Remember to write down all of your observations, your successes, your failures, the recommendations of friends and family, your frustrations, and your favorite anecdotes. Make images and sketches and even engage in some creative writing if the moment moves you. On a cold midwinter day, pulling down your garden journal from the shelf will bring a smile to your face, fond memories to the family, and hope for the seasons yet to come!

A welcoming garden

GARDEN RESOURCES

EXTENSION SERVICES

For information on plants, insects, soil testing, and various other garden topics, look up the university extension offices in your home state. Some examples:

University of Vermont:
https://www.uvm.edu/extension

Rutgers University:
https://njaes.rutgers.edu/extension/

Penn State:
https://extension.psu.edu/

University of Maryland:
https://extension.umd.edu

GARDEN CONSERVATION

National Wildlife Federation:
https://certifiedwildlifehabitat.nwf.org/

Xerces Society—Habitat Planning:
https://xerces.org/pollinator-conservation/habitat-restoration/planning

Xerces Society—Pollinator Habitat:
https://xerces.org/pollinator-conservation/yards-and-gardens

National Audubon—Bird-Friendly Yards:
https://www.audubon.org/magazine/july-august-2013/
how-create-bird-friendly-yard

National Audubon—Habitat Certification:
https://www.audubon.org/news/
protocols-bird-friendly-habitat-management-certification

GARDEN TOOLS

Garden Tool Company:
https://www.gardentoolcompany.com/collections/all-garden-tools

Grow Organic:
https://www.groworganic.com/collections/tools-equipment

Tractor Supply:
https://www.tractorsupply.com/tsc/catalog/garden-hand-tools

SEEDS

Grow Organic:
https://www.groworganic.com/collections/non-gmo-and-organic-seeds

Back to the Roots:
https://backtotheroots.com/collections/organic-seeds

Botanical Interests:
https://www.botanicalinterests.com/collections/organic

EPILOGUE

A FUTURE FARM DREAM

On a recent morning out in my garden, I celebrated the day. It was cooler than it had been over the past several weeks, and the sun was just reaching the veggie plot that I was inspecting for potential harvest. My backyard chickens called from the run, asking to be let out for a morning stretch. A catbird paused on the cedar lattice, surveying for pokeweed berries next to the garden (I was happy it passed up the ripening figs on our small tree across the yard). The smell of the tomato plants and moist soil brought a smile to my face, and I entered a daydream that was occurring more and more over the past few growing seasons.

I could be a farmer, I thought to myself. Early-morning visits out in the fields, checking on plants and animals. Studying the weather, the soil, and the occasional plant problem. I love experimenting with new seeds and plants and enjoy devising ways to work around challenges in my garden. My plans include a couple of small greenhouses, where I could

extend the growing season and maybe teach a few classes to kids from the local school. I would specialize in organic herbs, honey from a few beehives, and free-range eggs from a manageable-sized flock of hens. I would keep a journal and document the interactions among people, crops, the soil, the weather, and the wildlife. This is my romantic idea of a garden farmer.

Afterall, I have experience working on a farm. One of my first jobs was as a farmhand in my younger days. Weighed down with a metal bucket tied around my waist, I signed on for eight-hour shifts of picking blueberries in the hot South Jersey sun. The snack breaks were sweet, and my skin tanned while my fingers stained purple. I was paid on the basis of how fast I picked. If I needed a day off to fish with my friends, the farmer who owned the field approved, since he enjoyed a good day of fishing as well, and he would always throw a few extra dollars in my pay at the end of the summer for my dedicated efforts and efficient harvest.

During college I worked my winter breaks at a Christmas tree farm. Following around families who cherished the idea of picking out just that perfect tree for the season, I would harvest and haul their selection to their car and secure the tree to the roof. If the day was slow, we would cut fresh greens and make wreaths; I still do this every December for friends and family. Despite the near frostbite and the sappy residues that would accumulate on my clothes, I think back on those days with fondness. A 40-foot eastern white pine growing in my garden as I write this passage is a tree I transplanted from the ground at this farm.

Chickens in the garden

Garden gifts

In the environmental science classes I teach, I always enjoy the agriculture unit. I am fascinated by the history of agriculture, the diversity of crops grown around the world, the various innovations that have advanced our food-producing abilities, and, especially, the interest that more and more people seem to be taking in how their food is grown and what that means for their health and the well-being of the planet. It is this connection between farms and public education that I feel is particularly important so that people can have healthful food while the natural world supports every other species as well.

Embrace your inner farmer! Plan, plant, tend, harvest, share, and enjoy! Here's to our next garden adventure!

Garden harvest

GLOSSARY

adaptation: Any feature or behavior that makes an organism suited to its environment
apiary: A place where bees are kept; a collection of beehives
biodiversity: The variety of life in the world, in an ecosystem or specific location
cold stratification: Exposing seeds to a period of cold temperatures with low moisture
community supported agriculture (CSA): A farm supported by individuals within the community
compost: Decayed organic material used as plant fertilizer
conservation: Prevention of wasteful use of a natural resource
cover crop: A crop grown for the protection and enrichment of the soil
crop rotation: The practice of moving the location of crops grown to improve soil and plant health
cultivate: To prepare and use land for crops or gardening
decomposition: The state or process of rotting/decay of organic material, resulting in the release of nutrients
detritivore: An animal that feeds on dead organic material (detritus)
ecosystem services: The various benefits provided to nature and humans by biodiversity and ecosystem processes
foodshed: A geographic location that produces food for a particular region and population
germination: The development of a plant from a seed or spore after a period of dormancy
hardening: The process that allows a plant to transition from protected indoor space to the harsher conditions of outdoor space
hardiness zone map: A map that displays the geographic areas with a certain average temperature that indicates potential planting and growth of plants/crops
heirloom varieties: Older varieties of plants/crops that have been passed down from generation to generation
industrial agriculture: Modern farming approaches that require a lot of resources to maximize production of crops; resources include pesticides, fertilizers, water, and energy

inoculation: (regarding fungi) Introducing a small number of cells, spores, or tissue into a medium that will result in the new growth of fungi

intercropping: The practice of growing more than one crop/plant in the same space

invasive species: A species, often not native to an area, that causes ecological or economical harm to an area

invertebrate: Any of a large diversity of animals that lack a backbone

irrigation: The supply of water to land or crops to increase growth and production

leaf litter: Leaves and other plant materials that form a layer on top of the soil; can be used a natural fertilizer and is an important source of nutrients

microbes: Microorganisms such as bacteria or fungi; essential for healthy soil in farms and gardens

microclimate: The climate of a small or restricted area that is different from the surrounding climate; often due to a particular features of the space

monocropping: Growing only one crop on a given plot or farm; often year after year

mycelium: The vegetative part of a fungi forming extensive white filaments, usually underground

nutrients: A substance that provides nourishment essential for growth and maintenance of life

organic: (in agriculture) Food grown and processed using no synthetic pesticides or fertilizers

pH: A measurement of the acidity or alkalinity of water or soil (or other material); measured from 0 (most acidic) to 14 (most alkaline)

pesticide: A chemical substance used to kill insects, weeds, or other problematic species

photosynthesis: The process by which plants (and algae and some bacteria) produce food by using light energy and carbon dioxide and water

plumage: The feathers of a bird

pollination: The transfer of pollen from the male part of a flower (stamen) to the female part of the flower (carpel) by wind or animal, potentially leading to fertilization

rain garden: A garden located in a low-lying area that collects rainwater runoff, allowing water to infiltrate into ground; can reduce pollution from runoff

seedling: A young plant that has grown from a germinated seed

smoker: A device used to generate smoke to calm honeybees in a hive

spawn (fungal): Material used to transfer fungal mycelium to a new substrate; used for mushroom cultivation

sustainable farming: Practices that enhance environmental health, biodiversity, and natural resources while providing healthful food or other crops

symbiosis: The interaction of two organisms in close association in a habitat or ecosystem; can be parasitic, in which one benefits at the expense of the other, or mutual, in which both benefit from the relationship

USDA (United States Department of Agriculture): The federal department that oversees and regulates farming, ranching, and forestry in the United States

weed: A plant not valued, or deemed problematic, where it is growing

GARDEN FIELD NOTES

Start your own gardening journal by writing your observations and ideas on the following pages.

_____

_____

_____

_____

_____

_____

_____

_____

_____

_____

_____

_____

_____

_____

_____

_____

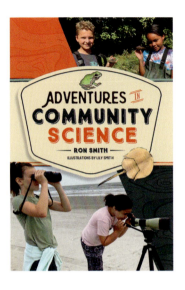

Adventures in Community Science: Notes from the Field and a How-To Guide for Saving Species and Protecting Biodiversity

Young readers and educators explore various community science projects through natural history, journal entries, and sample data sets. One part nature journal and one part call to action, these studies and surveys will inspire readers to engage the natural world through hands-on exploration.

978-0-7643-6575-1
$14.99

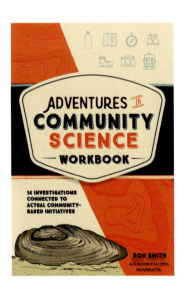

Adventures in Community Science Workbook: 14 Investigations Connected to Actual Community-Based Initiatives

An investigative, interdisciplinary activity book that offers classroom students, homeschooled children, and visitors to nature centers and parks the opportunity to build their collaborative, scientific skills through data sets, natural-history study, and creative lessons.

978-0-7643-6576-8
$9.99